The Confessions
of
Frederick the Great
and
The Life of
Frederick the Great

By
Heinrich von Treitschke

Now for the First Time Translated into English

Edited, with a Topical and Historical Introduction
by
Douglas Sladen

With a Foreword by
Geo. Haven Putnam

G. P. Putnam's Sons
New York and London
The Knickerbocker Press
1915

Copyright, 1915
BY
G. P. PUTNAM'S SONS

The Knickerbocker Press, New York

PREFACE

THE origin of the gospel of inhumanity preached by von Bernhardi in his *Germany and the Next War* is to be found in the *Confessions of Frederick the Great*, which came into my hands accidentally a short time ago. The Rev. Graham McElroy, whom I met at a friend's house, who had noticed the resemblance, lent me an eighteenth century duodecimo containing an English translation of the first five "Mornings" of the *Confessions*, which up till then were unknown to me. And about the same time the editor of *The Globe* showed me the proof of an article which he had commissioned upon this book. It was a learned and intuitive paper, and a perusal of it and the book made me explore the subject at the British Museum. There I found the other two "Mornings," in another little eighteenth-century volume in their original French, and one of them, the highly important "Morning" which deals with Finance, had apparently never been translated into English on account of its banality.

Banal it is, but it contributes not a little to proving that the *Confessions* really were written by Frederick, for it sets forth, so naturally that one can almost hear Frederick saying the words, his nostrums for improving the administration and the yield of the Prussian taxes.

But intrinsic evidence is not necessary, for the manuscript of the *Confessions* in French has been preserved in Frederick's own handwriting, and if it were necessary, I have the opinion of the accomplished French scholar to whom I sent, to be typed, my translation of "Mornings" VI. and VII. When I met her, I asked if she knew what she had been typing. "No," she replied, "and what is more, I cannot be certain whether the translation is from the French or from the German"—the fact being that Frederick, writing in French, was unable to divest himself of Germanisms.

Even had von Bernhardi not openly confessed, by allusion, his obligations to Frederick, no one who had read the two books could fail to perceive that the seed of *Germany and the Next War* is to be found in the extremely amusing and shameless *Confessions* of Frederick the Great. It is obvious in all its nakedness.

And since von Bernhardi constantly admits his indebtedness to Treitschke, the historian of the Prussification of Germany, it seemed to me that I could offer no more interesting commentary on Frederick's *Confessions* than a translation of what Treitschke wrote about the great Frederick. This, like most of Treitschke's works, had never been translated into English. It proved very difficult to translate, and as my knowledge of German is slight, Miss Louise Scheerer made a literal

Preface

translation of it, which I transposed, as far as I was able, into current phraseology. Mr. Sidney Whitman, the learned author of our chief books about Bismarck, who is second to no English writer on contemporary Germany and Austria, had almost completed explaining the phrases which baffled us, when he introduced Dr. Oscar Levy, the editor of the great eighteen-volume translation of Nietzsche, and the chief authority on Nietzsche in Great Britain. Dr. Levy has most generously gone through our entire translation to see that no mistranslations have crept in.

It may be taken, therefore, that whatever the literary faults, due entirely to me, may be, the translation is accurate, a matter of immense importance where Treitschke, who is almost as difficult to translate as Carlyle would be, is concerned. Treitschke, like Carlyle, is a great word-coiner and word-joiner, and pours forth torrents of ideas. But he is not more reliable than Macaulay, for he generally applied a similarly encyclopædic knowledge with the partisanship of an advocate rather than the justice of a judge.

What sort of man Frederick was I shall endeavour to show in an introduction more within the comprehension of a plain man than he would be likely to find Treitschke's pregnant analysis of Frederick's share in Prussification.

I shall not detain the reader by specifying the actual passages in the *Confessions* which are paralleled by von Bernhardi, but shall prefer to point out how Frederick's unblushing disciple has put into practice their Royal Larkinism, their gospel of *Tuum est meum*.

D. S.

LONDON, December, 1914.

FOREWORD

THERE is a sharp conflict of opinion in regard to the causation of, or the responsibility for, the great struggle that is now desolating Europe and that has even extended to the furthermost coast of Asia. It is my own opinion, an opinion which is I believe held by the great majority of Americans, that this conflict will go down to history as the war of German aggression. The war has been described as the natural expression of what has come to be known as the Hohenzollern spirit and as the necessary result of the Hohenzollern policy. Berlin and London are at this time in accord on very few matters, but it is possible that this definition in regard to the inevitability of the European war under the conditions existing would be accepted in both capitals.

Those who are studying the war with reference to its causes and its probable results, and particularly those who are in the position of Americans and can investigate the war conditions without reference to the safety, or at least to the immediate safety, of their own homes, may naturally be interested, therefore, in tracing the history of what is called the Hohenzollern spirit and the development of this all-important Hohenzollern policy.

The Hohenzollern family has shown a full measure of vitality and on the whole of persistence of purpose; but, like all historic families the record of which extends over centuries, its successive personalities have varied very greatly in individual force and in effectiveness, and also in the nature and extent of their contributions to the success of the family in the development of the realms over which they came to rule and in extending its influence upon the world outside of those realms.

When, in the thirteenth century, Conrad of Hohenzollern, at that time Burggrave of Nuremberg, directed his political ambitions toward North Germany, he doubtless indulged in the usual visions of personal glory for himself and for his family. He could hardly, however, have looked forward to the position that was to be secured, at the close of centuries of effort, by his Hohenzollern descendants. The first historic reference that we find to the Hohenzollerns is connected with the name of Tasselin, who was active in the time of Charlemagne, but the family of the Zollern Castle comes into actual history only with the *wanderjahr* and the promotion of Burggrave Conrad. The beginning of the political power of the family may be said to date from 1568 when the duchy of Prussia was made hereditary in the House of Hohenzollern. It is the state developed from the duchy of Prussia that

Foreword

to-day dominates the Empire of Germany and that is fighting for the domination of Europe. The real founder of the kingdom of Prussia and of the Empire that has developed from that kingdom was not the first King, Frederick I, to whom the crown came in 1701, but his father the great Elector of Brandenburg. It was the Elector whose force of will and organizing capacity instituted what might be called the Prussian system, under which the resources of Brandenburg and Prussia were later made so wonderfully effective. The son of the Elector, the first King, did not impress himself upon the history of the time; while the service of the grandson, Frederick William I, was rendered in the form of saving up the resources in men and in money which were to be utilized so effectively by his son Frederick II, known as Frederick the Great.

The *Confessions* of Frederick were brought into print in an English edition in the latter part of the eighteenth century, shortly after the death of the King. In the frank obliviousness of any moral responsibility for human, or at least for royal, action, they recall the famous letters written by Lord Chesterfield for the guidance of his godson. There is, of course, a wide difference between the subjects considered by the two writers. The Englishman is giving counsel, based upon his own experience, for the success of his godson in social and political life, while the Prussian is impressing upon the young man who is to succeed him in the control of the kingdom the principles and the policies by which such kingdom should be maintained and developed. The letters are, however, curiously similar in their frank—one may say their naïve—disregard of moral principle as having anything to do either with the life of an English courtier or with the work of a Prussian King.

With this utterance of King Frederick has been associated a biographical and critical study written by the historian Treitschke, who made himself the exponent of the Hohenzollern spirit. From these two works, so different in purpose and in character, the reader is able to secure a distinct and fairly complete picture of the nature, the methods, and the policy of Frederick the Great. He secures further an indication of the principles upon which Frederick's successor, William II, appears to have planned the policy of Germany with the purpose of shaping the destinies of Europe. In his *Confessions*, Frederick remarks that

it is not to eminence in virtues that our family owes its aggrandizement. The greater part of our princes have been rather remarkable for misconduct, but it was chance and circumstances that have been of service.

He complains that

his kingdom is not well situated and that the different portions of the territory are not well arranged to each other. They are dispersed or divided in such manner that they cannot mutually assist each other.

The series of wars waged by Frederick had for their purpose the correction of this troublesome irregularity of boundary; and he succeeded, through the appropriation from his neighbours of the pieces of territory needed, in rounding out the dominions of Prussia.

The principles set forth by Frederick for the guidance of his nephew in the development of the Prussian realm, principles based upon the King's own experience, are affirmed in substance one hundred and fifty years later, in their philosophic relation, by Nietzsche. Says Nietzsche:

A good war will sanctify any cause. . . . Active sympathy for the weak is more dangerous to the human race than any crime. . . . At the bottom of all distinguished races, the beast of prey is not to be mistaken. To demand of strength that it should not assert itself as strength, that it should not be a will to oppression, a will to destruction, a will to domination, that it should not be athirst for foes and opposition and triumph, is precisely as senseless as to demand of weakness that it assert itself as strength.

A writer in a recent number of the *Unpopular Review* points out that Frederick was no hypocrite.

There never was a straighter monarch. He merely had the Prussian conscience. His suspicions of foreign powers are facts to be acted on, and he feels that an act which in a foreign nation is that of a cut-throat is, when done in the behoof of Prussia, not only justified, but holy.

(We may compare with this the "scrap of paper," and the havoc wrought in Belgium for holy ends.)

The article in the *Review* says further:

This kind of conscience is general in grim, martial, partially civilized nations which have been forged tough in the struggle for existence. Such peoples trust to their suspicions and their hates and they readily justify their own worst aggressions as simple anticipatory measures of self-defence. If such a nation can acquire the inventions and the resources of civilization without permitting civilization to abate these suspicions and hates, or impair the conviction that the nation can do no harm, such a nation will be more formidable in arms than any truly civilized state can hope to be.

Frederick tells his nephew that "religion is absolutely necessary in the state," but goes on to say that "it would not be wise in a King to have any religion himself. . . ."

There is nothing [he says] that tyrannizes more over the head and heart than religion, because it neither agrees with our passions nor with those great political views by which a monarch ought to be guided. The true religion of a prince is his interest and his glory.

Foreword

Under the heading of "Justice," Frederick emphasizes with his nephew that,

we must do justice to all men, and especially to our own subjects when so doing would not overset or interfere with our own rights or wound our own authority. There ought to be no sort of equality between the right of the monarch and the right of the subject or slave.

Under the heading of "Politics," he expresses the opinion that,

to cheat or to deceive one's fellow-creatures is a mean and criminal action. . . . The term that has been invented to describe such action is *Politics*. . . . I understand by this, dear nephew, that we are ever to try to cheat others. This is the way to secure the advantage, or, at least, to be on a footing with the rest of mankind; for you may rest persuaded that all the states of the world run the same career. . . . Never be ashamed of making alliances, but do not commit the stupid fault of not abandoning these alliances whenever it is to your interest so to do. . . . Stripping your neighbours is only to take away from them the means of doing an injury to yourself.

In a later chapter on what might be called "Applied Politics," the King tells the nephew that he "will not trouble him with" a demonstration of the validity of the pretensions under which Silesia had been seized, but that he had "taken care to have these duly established by his orators." "It is good policy," continues Frederick, "to be always attempting something, and in any case to be perfectly persuaded that we have a right to everything that suits us." "To form alliances for one's advantage is a great maxim of state, and there are no powers that can excuse themselves for a neglect of this. . . ." It is evident, however, that "an alliance should be broken as soon as it becomes prejudicial. I have already, my dear nephew, told you that politics and villainy are almost synonymous terms." This is quite in line with the teachings of Chesterfield.

When a stranger comes to your court, overwhelm him with civilities, and take pains to have him constantly near you. . . . This is the best way to keep concealed from him the defects of your government.

One would suppose that in this counsel Frederick was foreshadowing the ingenious plan of his successor William II for the establishment of exchange professorships.

Under the heading of "Military Counsel," in his account of the management of his army Frederick says:

I ascertained who in the army were regular bandits. . . . I closed my eyes to the oppressions committed by the general officers. . . . They work for me in working for themselves.

Visitors to Germany have been impressed, and particularly since 1871, with the general recogni-

Foreword

tion insisted upon by the military authorities, and accepted by the populace at large, of the superiority of the profession of arms. It is the belief of not a few friends of Germany that the dominating manner which actuates the army officers, and particularly those of Prussia, is not merely an annoyance to the civilians, but has proved a very bad training for the officers themselves, but this right to dominate has been insisted upon consistently in a long series of utterances of William II. In like manner Frederick says, "Always confer an air of superiority on the profession of arms."

A century and a half later, Nietzsche writes: "The future of German civilization rests on the sons of the Prussian officers." It is because this principle was accepted by Frederick and has been developed by Frederick's successors, that the word has gone forth to Germany and the world that the German officer was something sacrosanct, and that for the safety and the development of the state he must be permitted to dominate the civilian. He was to be accepted as an awe-inspiring representative of the Kaiser. Any temporary annoyance to the civilian population was to be fully atoned for later by the glorious success of "the Day."

The *Confessions* close with a chapter having to do with "Finance," in which Frederick places before his nephew with considerable detail his principles of taxation and the methods under which he managed the resources of the realm. It is evident from a study of these tables that the King was a wonderful organizer, and a good man of business. One may judge that he was a difficult bargainer to get the better of or to impose upon. It is probable that for the purpose of building up the realm of Prussia, a better instructor than Frederick could not have been found. It may be questioned to-day, however, whether the principles and policies which have been handed down to his successors by this the greatest of the Hohenzollerns may not in the end prove disastrous to Germany.

Macaulay, analyzing the successive wars of annexation of Frederick, says that "his selfish rapacity gave the signal to his neighbours. . . . His example quieted their sense of shame." The historian proceeds:

On the head of Frederick is to be placed all the blood which was shed in a war that raged during many years and in every quarter of the globe. . . . The evil produced by his wickedness was felt in lands where the name of Prussia was unknown; and in order that Frederick might rob a neighbour whom he had sworn to defend, black men fought on the coast of Coromandel and red men scalped each other by the Great Lakes of North America.

The historian Treitschke on the other hand finds Frederick a hero after his own heart. He takes the same actions that had formed the text for Macaulay's excoriation and describes these in such manner as to show that in his judgment they were necessary for the development of Prussia and of Germany, and for the proper carrying out of the destiny of the Hohenzollerns. Says Treitschke:

Since the days of Gustavus Adolphus, the Lion of the Midnight Sun, Germany had had no picture of a hero to whom the entire nation could look up with awe. . . . Frederick strode through the middle of the Great Powers and forced the Germans to believe again in the wonder of heroism. . . . He was a German, and the mainspring in this mighty nature is the ruthless, terrible German directness.

The historian remarks that

not without arbitrariness Frederick arranged the facts of history according to a one-sided view, but one-sidedness, turned towards life and light, is, after all, the privilege of the creative genius. . . .

And again:

Frederick recognized that it had become a necessity to enlarge the territory of his state . . . and his policy was to lift the new German state into expansion and power through the frightfulness of its weapons.

It may be noted that this term "frightfulness" has been utilized to-day in the instructions given to the generals who are occupying conquered territories in Belgium and in eastern France, as necessary for the terrorizing of the people.

Treitschke finds no ground for criticizing his hero "because no treaty or league could make him resign the right of deciding for himself," that is to say, of selecting his own time for the breaking of his obligation. The historian points out, and with truth, that as early as 1756 Frederick had recognized that the continuing issue in Germany was whether it was to accept the supremacy of Prussia or of Austria. The question was decided for Germany a century later at Königgrätz by William I, Bismarck, and Moltke. The soldier, reading the account of the campaigns of the Seven Years' War, cannot withhold a full measure of admiration for the pluck, the persistence, the patience, and the genius which carried the little army intact through defeats, and through victories which were hardly less exhausting than defeats, and which saved the existence of the little kingdom; but the courage of the troops and the genius of their leader had, of course, nothing whatsoever to do with the morality of the cause for which they were fighting, a cause which for the larger portion of all the campaigns of Frederick was simply the appropriation of the territory of his neighbour.

Treitschke writes in reference to the "educational power of war" that the "alert self-reliance of the Prussians contrasted strongly with the inoffensive kindly modesty of the other Germans." The quality that Treitschke terms "self-reliance" has in later years been described by those less sympathetic with the Prussian spirit as self-

Foreword

sufficiency or dominating arrogance. The truth of either definition depends, of course, upon the point of view.

Treitschke says, naïvely,

that there then dawned upon Frederick the idea of the partition of Poland. It was his purpose to combat the grabbing land-greed of Russia. . . . The Poles were, in any case, deserving of no sympathy, for [says Treitschke] they were distinguished above all the nations of Europe by an insolent disregard of the rights and the nationalities of others.

In Treitschke's reference to the organization given by Frederick to his army, he refers to the decision to place the officers' commissions exclusively in the hands of the nobility. He goes on to say:

In the noble officers' corps there arose an aristocratic arrogance (*Junkersinn*), which soon became more intolerable to the people than the coarse roughness of earlier times.

It is the belief of many that this characteristic of the corps of noble Prussian officers is stronger and more troublesome in the twentieth century than it was in the eighteenth.

Treitschke writes with full approval of Frederick's upholding of Christian toleration. He cites this as an old Prussian policy, and quotes Frederick's own words, "the people's conceptions of God and godly things cannot be made subject to a coercive law."

The defenders of the war policy of Germany of to-day contend that undue weight has been given to the utterances of the historian Treitschke, of the military scientist Bernhardi, and of the philosopher Nietzsche. When, however, it is possible to make clear that the germ of the teachings of historian, philosopher, and militarist is to be found in the recorded utterances of the greatest of the Hohenzollerns, and when the Hohenzollern of to-day says frankly that he is doing what he can to carry out the ideals of the King who made Prussia a European power, it is not inaccurate to contend that the spirit and principles of Frederick, Treitschke, Nietzsche, and Bernhardi are expressed by the policies and enforced by the military power of William II.

Frederick did not dread the antagonism of his neighbours and had no fear of their criticism. He was prepared to realize that he could hardly expect friendliness of feeling from the states whose territory had been despoiled to make Prussia greater. The defenders of the policy of Kaiser William II point out that Germany is surrounded by a "steel ring of enemies," states which are opposed to her natural development. Every nation is, of necessity, in touch with neighbouring nations; and whether these nations are to hold one of their neighbours in friendship or in enmity depends, of course, largely, if not chiefly, upon her own conduct and upon her observance in international relations of the principles of justice or of fair consideration. It is difficult to imagine that Germany should expect sympathetic friendship from Denmark (one third of whose territory had been snatched from her in 1864), or from France after the appropriation of Alsace-Lorraine and the institution in old French Lorraine of the great fortress of Metz threatening as it were with a mailed fist the heart of France. If Germany succeeds in the present struggle so that the annexation of Belgium as a province of the Empire (*Reichsland*) may be confirmed, it is hardly to be expected that for generations to come the Belgians, devastated by ruthless invasion and by the official burning of their cities, left in starvation through the appropriation of their food supplies, and crushed with heavy indemnities, some of which were imposed even after the territory had in form become a part of the German Empire, can regard with affection or with a feeling of loyal relation, their new rulers.

The reign of Frederick is a great example of the results of doctrines of efficiency carried to the nth power without scruples or limitations, or consideration for the rights of others. It is this Hohenzollern ideal of efficiency which has produced the finest fighting machine that the world has ever seen, and which has placed back of that machine the magnificently organized resources of a great Empire. It is for Europe to decide whether it will permit itself to be dominated by the ideals, the policy, and the methods of the Hohenzollerns

GEO. HAVEN PUTNAM.

NEW YORK, January, 1915.

CONTENTS

	PAGE
PREFACE	iii
FOREWORD	vii
INTRODUCTION	1

MORNING THE FIRST:

ORIGIN OF OUR FAMILY	35
THE SITUATION OF MY KINGDOM . .	37
OF THE SOIL OF MY TERRITORIES . .	38
OF THE MANNERS OF THE INHABITANTS .	38

MORNING THE SECOND:

ON RELIGION	40

MORNING THE THIRD:

ON JUSTICE	49

MORNING THE FOURTH:

ON POLITICS	54
ON PRIVATE POLITICS	55
ON LITERATURE	59
CONDUCT IN THE SMALLER MATTERS OF LIFE	61
AS TO DRESS	62
AS TO PLEASURES	63

Contents

	PAGE
MORNING THE FIFTH:	
ON POLITICS OF THE STATE	66
PRINCIPLE THE FIRST—OF SELF-PRESERVATION AND AGGRANDIZEMENT	66
PRINCIPLE THE SECOND—ON ALLIANCES	69
PRINCIPLE THE THIRD — OF INSPIRING RESPECT AND FEAR	71
MORNING THE SIXTH:	
MILITARY	74
MORNING THE SEVENTH:	
CONCERNING FINANCE	93
THE MEMORIAL OF THE COUNCIL	94
SUBSIDIES	98
MEMORANDUM FROM THE PROVINCE OF MINDEN	99
EXCISE DUES	101
THE REPLY OF THE PROVINCE OF MAGDEBURG	101
INSTRUCTIONS TO THE BURGOMASTERS OF MAGDEBURG	103
INSTRUCTIONS TO THE BURGOMASTERS OF VILLAGES	105
CONCERNING SALT	105
METHOD OF WORKING	106
MEMORANDUM SENT TO THE PROVINCE OF MINDEN	107

Contents

	PAGE
TOBACCO	108
FORESTRY	109
PROVINCE OF MINDEN — REPORT SENT TO THE COUNCIL BY THE SURVEYOR	110
SCHEDULE OF THE DISTRICT OF ——.	113
MEMORANDUM OF THE POSTAL SERVICE TO THE KING	114
POST-HOUSES	115
STAMP OFFICE AND REGISTRATION OF DEEDS	117
STAMPED PAPER	117
MODUS OPERANDI	118
CUSTOMS-DUTY ON FOREIGN GOODS	119
OCTROI DUTIES IN THE TOWNS	120
ARMY	123
TABLE SHOWING REPAYMENT OF DEBT	125

LIFE OF FREDERICK THE GREAT . . . 128
  BY HEINRICH VON TREITSCHKE

Introduction

INTRODUCTION

CARLYLE'S million words about Frederick the Great are too tedious for this impatient century, and, though there is an admirable life of Frederick by Mr. W. F. Reddaway in the *Heroes of the Nations* series, comparatively few English people are acquainted with the great King's frank effrontery and biting mother-wit, which are so conspicuous in his *Confessions*. Here are a few of the flowers which Mr. Reddaway has gathered.

His father made him marry Elizabeth of Brunswick-Bevern. Frederick's comment was:

When all is said and done, there will be one more unhappy princess in the world. [Twice he declared:] I shall put her away as soon as I am master. Am I of the wood out of which they carve good husbands? I love the fair sex, my love is very inconstant; I am for enjoyment, afterwards I despise it. I will keep my word, I will marry, but that is enough; *Bon jour, Madame, et bon chemin.*

. . . .

Good counsel does not come from a great number [was his maxim]. Newton could not have discovered the law of gravitation if he had been collaborating with Leibnitz and Descartes.

. . . . . .

After a sweeping measure of confiscation, which compelled the clergy to practise apostolic poverty, he wrote to Voltaire: "We free them from the cares of this world so that they may labour without distraction to win the heavenly Jerusalem which is their true home."

. . . . .

"I know very well," wrote Frederick to his brother, Prince Henry, as another King of Prussia might very well be imagined writing to another brother Henry, "that it is only our interest which makes it our duty to act at this moment, but we must be very careful not to say so."

And to that same brother he wrote:

I, who am already more than half beyond this world, am forced to double my wisdom and activity, and continually keep in my head the detestable plans that this curséd Joseph begets afresh with every fresh day. I am condemned to enjoy no rest before my bones are covered with a little earth.

. . . . .

"If there is anything to be gained by being honest, let us be honest; if it is necessary to deceive, let us deceive."

. . . . . .

That was the Frederick who wrote the *Con-*

fessions which were first published in his lifetime in 1766, and never disowned by him. The nephew to whom he wrote was his successor. He tells his descent in the first "Morning." He was only the third King of Prussia, that monarchy having been established at the beginning of the eighteenth century, thirty-nine years before his accession, and when he came to the throne Prussia included neither Silesia nor West Prussia nor East Friesland. But he inherited what was of more value in the hands of a monarch with a mediæval conscience—namely, an overflowing treasury and an army of eighty-five thousand men, of whom the infantry, at any rate, were the best drilled in Europe, though his cavalry lacked the dash of the Austrian cavalry, and he could not afford decent artillery and engineers.

His father, Frederick William I, was a most unlovable man; he was a bully in his own home, a bully to his subjects, and as cowardly as a bully to his enemies. Though he had the best army in Europe, he was afraid to fight; he could only snarl and show his teeth when his kingdom was threatened, except where his avarice was touched, as when Charles XII of Sweden refused to pay him his bill for holding Stettin. This was more than he could stand, and in the joint attack on Sweden which followed, he secured spoils of great value, the mouths of the Oder. Treitschke has recorded in this volume what the Austrians said about Frederick William.

History has many unlovely things to record of Frederick William I, who was so miserly that the whole government of Prussia cost only fifty-five thousand a year, and the whole royal expenses less than eight thousand. His treatment of his eldest son—Frederick the Great, who might have been more like Alexander the Great if his father had been more like Alexander's father, Philip of Macedon, was stupid and abominable. The comparison is irresistible, for Philip, the rough northern neighbour of Athens, laid the foundation of his son's conquests, just as Frederick William, the rough northern neighbour of the Empire, laid the foundations of the conquests of Frederick the Great.

And here I must define the expressions "the Empire" and "German," which will come so often into these pages. It is incorrect to call it the "German Empire." There never was a German Emperor actually so-called until William the First was crowned at Versailles, less than half a century ago. Maria Theresa's father and husband, who come into these pages, were Holy Roman Emperors, the successors of the Emperors of the West, who in their turn had succeeded to the western half of the Empire founded by Augustus. And until Maria Theresa's father died, the Emperors for more than three hundred years in unbroken succession had been elected from the House of Habsburg, who ruled the Austrian monarchy.

As Emperors, the Holy Roman Emperors, even

Introduction 7

Charles the Fifth, had no dominions. They were merely the elected heads of the Holy Roman Empire, which was, in fact, a loose confederation of German electors and minor princes. But the Empire had so long been identified with the Austrian House that the hereditary Austrian dominions became confused with it.

This arrangement seemed likely to go on for ever, when Prussia, representing the Electorate of Brandenburg, interfered to get a Bavarian chosen to replace Maria Theresa's father; but, in point of fact, in 1806 the Holy Roman Emperor changed his title to Emperor of Austria, on the ground that the Holy Roman Empire was no longer either Holy, Roman, or an Empire.

Prussia was one of the States of the Empire, and up to the period of Frederick certain Prussian law-cases could be carried to the Imperial Courts. It was once suggested to Frederick the Great (perhaps prompted *à la* Cæsar) that he should have himself elected Emperor, but he dismissed the suggestion with characteristic cynicisms about the poverty of Prussia and the jealousy which it would provoke from the other States. The Empire was usually referred to as the *Holy Empire* and the word *German* was not used to signify a person of Teutonic race, but a member of some State included in the Holy Empire.

The great Frederick was born with humanistic ideas uppermost; he took up military studies to escape some of the awful bullying inflicted on him by his father, who hated him so that he tried to persecute the unhappy child into his grave. Only the creator of "Oliver Twist" could adequately describe the boyhood of Frederick the Great. Frederick had to do so many things to deceive his father that everyone thought that his interest and apparent progress in military studies were only clever pieces of acting. "I have just drilled, I drill, I shall drill," he wrote.

So cruel was the father, that the son at the age of eighteen attempted to flee from Prussia with his "chum" and confidant, the youthful Katte. They were arrested and flung into prison, and charged with high treason as military officers who had deserted. Katte, in spite of his acquittal by the court-martial appointed to try him, was executed—a refinement of cruelty—before his friend's eyes. Frederick, who had begged to die in Katte's place, fainted with anguish, and would have shared his fate but for the remonstrances of the Emperor. The ambassadors of other sovereigns joined in the protest, but probably weighed nothing in comparison.

Frederick William only listened to the Emperor as his technical lord, from whom he lacked the military courage to declare himself free. He pursued his revenge in various ways. When he was tired of treating his son as a convict, he made him marry a woman he did not like, the same woman who was giving a party at Schönhausen while Frederick was dying. How Frederick dreaded his father is proved by an anecdote told by Mr. Reddaway. "It was like a foretaste of death," he said, "when a hussar appeared to command his presence at Berlin."

I do not know whether to regard the letter which Frederick wrote to express his submission to his father as the bottom rung of sycophancy or as a masterpiece of irony and treachery interblent. I give Carlyle's translation:

"Cüstrin, 19th November, 1730.

"All-Serenest and All-graciousest Father,—

"To your Royal Majesty, my All-graciousest Father, have" (*i.e.*, "I have," if one durst write the "I"—*Carlyle*), "by my disobedience as Theiro" (Youro) "subject and soldier, not less than by my undutifulness as Theiro Son, given occasion to a just wrath and aversion against me. With the All-obedientest respect I submit myself wholly to the grace of my most All-gracious Father; and beg him, Most All-graciously to pardon me; as it is not so much the withdrawal of my liberty in a sad arrest (*malheureusen Arrest*), as my own thoughts of the fault I have committed, that have brought me to reason: Who, with all-obedientest respect and submission, continue till my end,

"My All-graciousest King's and Father's faithfully obedientest
"Servant and Son,"
"Friedrich."

But for his father's cruelty Frederick might have borne one of the most honoured names in history, instead of fouling his greatness as a conqueror, and his goodness as a father of his country, by reducing to a system for Prussia the treachery and statecraft of Cæsar Borgia. For it was Frederick the Great who founded the Borgia system, as avowed without shame by himself in his *Confessions*.

Fortunately or unfortunately for Frederick, the introducer of the Borgia system into Prussian politics, the Red Cross was still unknown, or he would doubtless have converted what victories the Austrians did win against him into defeats.

I hold that the responsibility for the treachery of Frederick the Great must be laid at the door of his father, because without a system of smooth lying he would have been murdered by that monster of cold-blooded cruelty.

With this single exception, Frederick comes well out of that hellish ordeal. The breaking of the flute which was his chief solace did not deprive him of his love of music. His flute remained to him what the harp of David was to Saul. He played it for a couple of hours a day while he was solving the stern problems of maintaining the national existence. The depriving a born writer of all books except the religious works which are to literature what stones are to bread, could not rob him of his desire to write or his literary gift. And, above all, the harshness with which his governors and gaolers were compelled to treat him, did not lead to his revenging himself upon them, when he

Introduction

came to have the power; and if he showed no affection to his wife, or anyone else on earth except the literary friends who were transfigured to him by Genius, this also may be put down to Frederick William, who not only gave him the gall of hatred instead of the honey of parental love, but deliberately cut him off from every soft breeze of affection. His sister Wilhelmina of Baireuth, his fellow-victim under the lash, reigned alone in the one tender spot in his heart.

His treachery included ingratitude and invested it with a halo in militarist eyes. It may be due to a distorted hero-worship for Frederick that the obligations of hospitality meant less to the Germans of Antwerp than to the Bedouin of the desert.

Frederick owed his life to Maria Theresa's father, yet when the Emperor died, he not only broke the Pragmatic Sanction, like the other monarchs who had signed it, but actually marched his armies into one of the girl-Princess's richest provinces in a time of profound peace and seized it. The acquisition of Silesia by Prussia was the first fruit of Frederick's treachery and brigandage —the brigandage extolled by von Bernhardi and practised by Potsdam. Treachery continued to sully his glory through every alliance of his reign. When his ally prospered too much, he went over to the enemy; it was no part of his policy to let France crush Austria or Austria crush France. And though England deserted him instead of his deserting England, he was offering to desert her for

France at the same time as he told the British Ambassador, on July 9, 1757, that "His Prussian Majesty said that as he resolved to continue firmly united with His [Britannic] Majesty, it would be to their mutual interest to think of terms of peace honourable and safe for both," etc.

When he was about to seize Silesia, he wrote to Podewils, who urged that some legal claim could be furbished up: "The question of right (*droit*) is the affair of ministers: it is your affair; it is time to work at it in secret, for the orders to the troops are given." And a quarter of a century later he wrote: "The jurisprudence of sovereigns is commonly the right of the Stronger."

I may now turn to the white side of his shield, and I turn with pleasure, for Frederick the Great was truly great—perhaps it would not be too much to say that no one has ever better deserved to be the national hero. For Prussia would have disappeared from the face of Europe if it had not been for his invincible soul, instead of being blessed with a vastly increased population and territory, and when he had made her position secure on the battle-field, he showed equal ability and resolution in rehabilitating commerce and agriculture in his ruined kingdom, which, after all his wars, he left free from debt. Nor does the total number of Prussian soldiers killed during his reign (180,000) contrast unfavourably with the losses of his descendant's armies in three months of the present war.

Introduction

While his wars lasted, every interest in his kingdom was sacrificed to the maintenance of his army. He did not pay any of the salaries to the civil employees of the Government from his ministers downwards, and he drained the country of nearly everything except the men employed in agriculture. But when war was over he employed his war-treasure of 25,000,000 thalers saved for the next campaign, and his war-horses—sixty thousand of them—and even the personnel of his army in restoring agriculture and re-starting industries, and he not only restored them, but set about "protecting" them.

Justice has not been rendered to his efforts in this direction, because most of our English lives of Frederick were written at a time when Free Trade was a fetish hymned by a chorus of half-persuaded hypocrites. Frederick saw, as the founders of the commercial greatness of the United States and the new German Empire saw, that the creation of industries depended on discouraging the importation of anything which could be manufactured in the country.

The success of Free Trade in England for so many years reminds me of what Barney Thompson, the bookmaker, said to one of the richest men in Australia, when the latter was being purse-proud in the bar of Mack's Hotel after the Geelong Races: "What's the good of you blowing about your money?—a log could have made it when you did."
At that time England's Free-traders had met with

no opposition, because no one else had anything to sell. Frederick's policy of protection prevented any of the sorely needed gold from leaving Prussia, and resulted in the establishment of all sorts of industries, notably those of an agricultural nature. These he helped in a novel way, and one which was of the highest importance, in a direction the value of which is not only realized still in Germany, but is *being reaped by Germany* at this moment.

Frederick, who, when his reign began, had a standing army of over eighty thousand men, raised from a population of little over two millions, saw that the amount of fighting men which any nation can put into the field must ultimately depend on its population, and Prussia's population was a widow's mite compared with Austria's. Accordingly he set to work to drain the marshes in his kingdom, and settle them with foreigners selected for their sturdiness, who were induced to accept the position by gifts of land and exemption from taxes for so many years. When he died Prussia contained five million inhabitants and seventy-five thousand square miles.

Frederick enjoys the further fame of being for his time a very humane prince. He reduced capital punishment as much as he could, and was never vindictive in repressing the indiscretions of well-disposed people.

This was of a piece with his extraordinary tolerance in religious matters. He allowed and pro-

Introduction 15

tected all creeds. He allowed his subjects to think as they liked, provided that they let him do as he liked. He not only restored the Lutherans, whose religion was the most dynastic of German religions, to all their liberties and privileges, but he welcomed the Jesuits when they were expelled from other countries, and found a use for them, because the supply of educators had run short in his wars. They acclimatized readily and impressed their methods even upon Prussian diplomacy.

In spite of all the ravages of his wars, he left Prussia immensely stronger than when he came to it; he laid the foundations upon which Bismarck reared the stately edifice of the new German Empire, the edifice filled to overflowing with wealth and prosperity by William II before he commenced the mad gamble now in progress—a gamble which recalls the prophecy of Mirabeau: "If ever a foolish prince ascends this throne we shall see the formidable giant suddenly collapse, and Prussia will fall like Sweden."

Frederick had few pleasures, except that of hospitality. He liked good living, and for his boon companions chose men of the highest intellect, chiefly Frenchmen. All the world knows of his almost passionate friendship for Voltaire, tempered as it was by Voltaire's contempt for Frederick except as a man of action, and Frederick's contempt for Voltaire except as a man of letters. When Voltaire came to Frederick as a political envoy, Frederick laughed at his diplomacy just as much as Voltaire laughed at the King's French verses. How malicious he could be about Voltaire will be found in the *Confessions*. D'Alembert was another friend of Frederick's, and he made Maupertuis the head of the Berlin Academy.

He was an indefatigable worker. When he died, it was said of him that his death was the only rest he ever took in his life. He certainly worked just as hard till the day of his death, for at eleven o'clock on his last night he ordered that he should be waked at four to work. But he died two hours too soon in the arms of the faithful valet who had been holding him up since midnight. The last words he spoke were to ask for his favourite dog, and to bid them cover it with a quilt.

Of his habits, Mr. W. F. Reddaway, the most readable of his biographers, wrote:

His habit was to rise at dawn or earlier. The first three or four hours of the morning were allotted to toilet, correspondence, a desultory breakfast of strong coffee and fruit, preceded by a deep draught of cold water flavoured with fennel leaves, and flute-playing as an accompaniment to meditation on business. Then came one or two hours of rapid work with his secretaries, followed by parade, audiences, and perhaps a little exercise. Punctually at noon Frederick sat down to dinner, which was always the chief social event of the day, and in later life became his only solid meal. He supervised his kitchen like a department of State. He considered and often amended the bill of fare, which contained the names of the cooks responsible for every dish. After dinner he marked with a cross the courses which had merited his approval. He inspected his household accounts with minute care and proved himself a master of domestic economy. The result was a dinner that Voltaire considered fairly good for a country in which there was no game, no decent meat, and no spring chickens.

Two hours, sometimes even four, were spent at table. Occasionally the time was devoted to the discussion of important business with high officials, but in general Frederick used it to refresh himself after his six or seven hours of toil. He ate freely, preferring highly spiced dishes, drank claret mixed with water, and talked incessantly. He was a skilful and agreeable host, putting his guests instantly at their ease, and by Voltaire's account, calling forth wit in others. After dismissing the company he returned to his flute, and then put the final touches to the morning's business. After this he drank coffee and passed some two hours in seclusion. During this period he nerved himself for fresh grappling with affairs by plunging into literature. In the year 1749 he produced no less than forty works. About six o'clock he was ready to receive his lector or to converse with artists and learned men. At seven began a small concert, in which Frederick himself used often to perform. Supper followed, but was brief, unless the conversation was of unusual interest. Otherwise the King went to bed at about nine o'clock and slept five or six hours. In later life he gave up suppers, but continued to invite a few friends for conversation. He then allowed himself rather more sleep. In his last years he lost the power to play his flute, and with it, apparently, the desire to hear music.

Mr. Reddaway adds that Frederick would not endure the presence of any woman—that, strictly speaking, he had no courtiers, and that his private secretary, Eichel, whom he worked like a slave, was never seen by any human being.

Frederick, who wrote a great deal more than most professional authors, could be really witty, though much of his wit consisted in drawing attention to other people's weaknesses—an easy performance for an absolute monarch, since most men can do it when they are too drunk to fear the consequences, which may be the origin of the saying *in vino veritas*.

Treitschke gives Frederick a very high rank as an author, but nothing which Frederick ever wrote is as readable in a translation as the *Confessions* which are given in this volume. The truth is that eighteenth century writings have to be excellent before they are readable, because they lack the human frankness of some other centuries. This frankness Frederick achieved only in the poorest of his literary productions, and for this reason Frederick's fame as an author is dead out of his own country; he is read only for the light which he throws upon that cynical, valiant soul which achieved one of the greatest works in the world—the creation of Prussia.

A few dates may be useful in following Treitschke's life of the great Prussian King, for Treitschke deals in *dicta* rather than dates.

Frederick was born on January 24, 1712. His

Introduction

mother was a sister of George II. He was eighteen years old when he tried to flee with Katte to France, and twenty-eight when his father died in 1740. He was married in 1733 to Princess Elizabeth of Brunswick-Bevern, related to the Austrian House. The Emperor Charles VI, Maria Theresa's father, died on October 20, 1740, and on December 16th Frederick entered Silesia with twenty-eight thousand men, with the intention of annexing it. His victory at Möllwitz, which practically gave him the country, was fought on April 10, 1741, but he was not confirmed in it till his victory of Chotusitz, May 17, 1742, which was followed on June 11th by the Peace of Breslau.

This is called the first Silesian war. In the next war against Austria, in 1744 (the second Silesian war), he took Prague, September 16, 1744, but had to abandon it shortly afterwards. He had his revenge at his great victories of Hohenfriedberg, on June 5, 1745, and Sohr, September 30, 1745, both against the Austrians, and Hennersdorf, November 23, 1745, against the Austrians and Saxons combined, while the Prince of Dessau defeated another Austrian and Saxon army at Kesselsdorf on December 15th. The second Silesian war was terminated by the Peace of Dresden, signed on Christmas Day, 1745.

On August 29, 1756, Frederick crossed the Saxon frontier and began the Seven Years' War. The indecisive battle of Lobositz was fought between Frederick and the Austrian Marshal

Browne, and before the end of the year he took possession of Saxony. On May 6, 1757, he won the battle of Prague, after enormous losses on both sides, and blockaded the city; but on June 18th he lost the great battle of Kollin, and had to raise the blockade and evacuate Bohemia. On November 5, 1757, he won the great battle of Rossbach, and a month later another supreme victory at Leuthen. On the 21st, Breslau capitulated to him, and a week later Liegnitz. But his General, Lehwaldt, had been defeated by the Russian General Apraxin at Gross-Jägersdorf on August 30th. In 1758 he marched into Moravia and besieged Olmütz, but was compelled to retreat owing to the capture of a convoy of three or four thousand wagons by the Austrian General Laudon; on August 25th he won the battle of Zorndorf over the Russians, which ended their campaign, but on October 14th he was surprised and heavily defeated by the Austrians at Hochkirch, and on the same day lost his sister, the Margravine of Baireuth.

But for the English subsidy of 4,000,000 thalers Frederick would have been starved out in 1759. On July 25th his army was defeated by the Russians at Kay, and on August 12th he saw his army utterly routed by the combined Austrians and Russians at Kunersdorf. He lost Dresden by surrender on September 24th, and on November 23d Finck and his army of 12,000 men laid down their arms at Maxen.

Introduction

In the western field things had gone better. Ferdinand of Brunswick had driven the French army across the Rhine on June 23, 1758, at Crefeld, and though the French took Frankfurt on January 2, 1759, and won a battle at Bergen on April 13, 1759, they were severely defeated at Minden, August 1, 1759.

On June 23, 1760, a Prussian corps was annihilated at Landeshut and Glatz capitulated on July 22d. But Frederick won a great victory over the Austrians under Laudon at Liegnitz on August 15th, and a hotly contested battle against the Austrians under Daun at Torgau on November 3d, though Laudon had surprised and captured the great fortress of Schweidnitz on October 1st. The condition of Prussia at the end of this year appeared hopeless; the army had declined to sixty thousand men, and even more in quality than in numbers. But on January 5, 1762, the Czarina Elizabeth of Russia died, and was succeeded by her nephew, Peter III, the husband of the great Catherine, who was an idolatrous admirer of Frederick and at once recalled the Russian army. Prussia and Russia signed a peace on May 5th, and an offensive and defensive alliance on June 8th, and Sweden made peace with Prussia at Hamburg on May 22d.

But in the interval the elder Pitt had been replaced as Prime Minister of England by the feeble Bute, who had but one desire—to terminate the war as soon as possible, and six months after

Peter III's succession the whole of Russia became so disgusted with him that on July 9, 1762, he was deposed by his wife, and a few days later strangled by her lover, Alexis Orloff. On July 21, 1762, Frederick won a battle over the Austrians at Burkersdorf, and in October captured Schweidnitz. Before the end of the year a truce was made which proved to be the end of the Seven Years' War—the Peace of Hubertusburg being signed on February 5, 1763.

Neither Frederick nor the Austrians gained an inch of territory in the Seven Years' War, but Austria failed in her object, which was to form a coalition to crush Frederick, and from this time forwards Prussia and Austria were equals and rivals.

It took Frederick twenty-three years, exactly half his reign, to arrive at this. The other half was spent almost entirely in peace, though there was a campaign, and gave Frederick the opportunity to show his powers of organizing agricultural and commercial enterprises and an economic system.

The principal events of the latter half of Frederick's reign were the Partition of Poland, the Bavarian Succession War, and the foundation of the League of Princes. In 1772, Frederick persuaded Austria and Russia to join him in the first Partition of Poland. His share was of great value to him, because until he obtained possession of Prussian Poland, East Prussia was detached from the rest of the kingdom.

Maria Theresa was only with great difficulty persuaded by her ambitious son to come into the arrangement. She complained that they had aimed at two incompatible objects at once, "to act in the Prussian fashion, and at the same time to preserve the semblance of honesty," to which Frederick sneeringly replied: "She is always weeping but always annexing."

The War of the Bavarian Succession in 1778 led to very little fighting. The main armies were unable to attack each other, and when the Czarina threatened to interfere on the Prussian side, Austria came to terms and made the Peace of Teschen, May 13, 1779. A year and a half later Maria Theresa died, leaving the restless Joseph without any steadying influence. To counter his attempts to increase the Imperial authority, Frederick gradually worked up not only the Protestant Princes of the Empire, but even the Catholic ecclesiastical States, to form the League of Princes (*Fürstenbund*), which was signed in the first instance by Brandenburg, Hanover, and Saxony only, on July 23, 1785. About a year afterwards, on August 17, 1786, Frederick died at the age of seventy-four.

This *Fürstenbund* was a fitting conclusion to his career, for it coincides approximately with the new German Empire.

Frederick found Prussia the smallest and weakest of the Great Powers, and left her equal to any of them. That should be his epitaph.

TREITSCHKE'S STUDY OF FREDERICK THE GREAT

Treitschke's study of Frederick would be interesting if it were only as a *tour de force* of character analysis. I think he overestimates the value of Frederick's *Anti-Machiavel* and his Letters on Patriotism, which are practically dead as far as the foreign reader is concerned; but in other respects his delineation of Frederick is comparatively free from the advocate's partisanship which depreciates Treitschke's value as an historian.

Whether Treitschke would have treated Frederick so impartially if he had been alive now is doubtful. To give an instance: a couple of pages after his magnificent summing-up of Frederick's greatness, he has a paragraph which is about the strongest condemnation of the present war which ever came from a German pen:

The love of peace of the House of Hohenzollern remained alive even in its greatest war-princes. Frederick valued power, but only as a means for the well-being and civilization of the nations; that it should be an end in itself, that the struggle for power as such should bestow historic fame, seemed to him as an insult to the honour of a sovereign. Therefore he wrote his passionate polemic-treatise against Machiavelli. Therefore, in his writings, he returned again and again to the terrible warning of Charles XII of Sweden. He might have felt secretly that in his own breast were working irresistible forces, which might lead him to similar errors, and was never tired of portraying the hollowness of objectless military fame. . . . Already in his impetuous youth he had made up his mind about the moral objects of power: "This State must become strong," he wrote at that time, "that it may play the lofty rôle of preserving peace only from love of justice, and not from fear. But if ever injustice, bias, and vice gain the upper hand in Prussia, then I wish the House of Brandenburg a speedy downfall. That says all."

To show how different from this is the undiluted Treitschke, one may quote a passage which has inspired numberless passages in von Bernhardi:

The educational power of war awakened again in these North-German races above all that rough pride which once inspirited the invaders of Italy (*Romfahrer*) and the conquerors of the Slavs in the Middle Ages.

And a few sentences later on he talks of the "descendants of those heroic nations, the Vandals and the Goths," in the same way as the present Emperor bade his soldiers emulate the Huns in an unfortunate speech which has given, through newspaper-headings, a severe blow to the German cause in America.

Yet Treitschke, like von Bernhardi, was, when he was not crusading, very sane and fair. He writes, for instance: "The alert self-reliance of the Prussians contrasted strongly with the inoffensive kindly modesty of the other Germans," just as the war news of to-day often contrasts the Saxons' or Bavarians' behaviour in Belgium or France with that of the Prussians. And a little lower down he says: "It was betrayed now in confident bragging, in the thousand satirical anecdotes of Imperial stupidity and Prussian Hussar strategisms." For which von Hindenburg's name will probably supply dictionaries with a new word.

Yet you can see in Frederick many signs of the anticipation of modern Prussian ideas which make him one of the most interesting figures in history, as he is one of the greatest figures at the present time. For in many ways the Prussia of to-day is the Prussia of Frederick's time come to life again. It was Frederick who said:

With such soldiers there is no risk: a General who in other armies would be considered foolhardy, is only considered with us as doing his duty. [And again he says:] It seems that Heaven has appointed the King to make all preparations which wise precautions before the beginning of a war demand. Who knows, if Providence has not reserved it for me to make a glorious use of these war means at some future time, and to convert them to the realization of the plans for which the foresight of my fathers intended them?

But I do not agree with Treitschke when he writes: "It was Frederick's work that . . . a third tendency should arise, a policy which was only Prussian, and nothing further: to it Germany's future belonged." And he writes later

Introduction

on: "Dohm concluded a clever pamphlet with these words: 'German and Prussian interests can never stand in one another's way.' The discerning mind of the old King was not moved by such dreams."

And we know how widely spread the distrust of Prussia was in Frederick's day, because Goethe, quoted by Treitschke, tells us that: "Even the humblest and weakest of the allied States, Weimar and Dessau, secretly discussed how they could protect themselves against their Prussian protector's lust of power."

When Treitschke talks of the moral justification of the treacherous seizure of Silesia, one is irresistibly reminded of the justification of the present war by von Bernhardi and others, for the beneficent results likely to happen from the spread of Prussian *Kultur*—the culture which it would be more reasonable to call the *Prussian vulture*. Treitschke damns Frederick's excuses for seizing Silesia with faint apologies:

He wished to spare Austria, and contented himself with bringing forward the most important of the carefully pondered pretensions of his House. Alone, without vouchsafing one word to the foreign Powers on the watch, with an overwhelming invading force, he broke into Silesia. Germany, used to the solemn reflections and cross-reflections of her Imperial lawyers, received with astonishment and indignation the doctrine that the rights of States were only to be maintained by active power.

Elsewhere in this book it will be seen how Frederick excelled himself on this occasion by ordering Podewils to find excuses because he had already given orders to his troops. The doctrine of the active power has been exploited for all it is worth by von Bernhardi in his *Germany and the Next War*.

Treitschke is not very convincing upon the subject of Poland. His complaints of "the Poles' horrible outrages in the Weichsel district, with that insolent disregard of the rights of others and the nationality of others which distinguishes the Poles above all the nations of Europe," leaves us cold, when our paper every morning brings news of fresh devastation in Poland. And the sentence in which Treitschke complains that: "Others repeated credulously what Poland's old confederates, the French, invented to stigmatize the partitioning Powers," simply kills Treitschke's reputation as an impartial historian. The world of honest men has never ceased to condemn the Partition of Poland, and hailed with almost religious delight Russia's proclamation that the ancient nation of the Poles should be reconstituted as a practically autonomous people under the shield of the Lion of the East, the great protector of Slav nationality. Any criticism, which Germany might have to make on the subject, is discounted by the fact that she at once proceeded to suggest a German parody of the movement, a highly improved province to embrace Russian Poland as well as Prussian Po-

Introduction 29

land. And any advantages, which may have been latent in this suggestion, are rendered difficult of realization by the *Belging* of Russian Poland.

The question of the Balance of Power, which is handled so destructively by von Bernhardi, comes up a good deal in Treitschke's life of Frederick the Great. I think von Bernhardi was right, but I arrive at my conclusions from a standpoint which he would hardly share. The European balance of power for many years has been like a wooden garden fence, whose bottom under the soil has rotted. From time to time—the last time was during and after the Balkan War against Turkey —Europe has been on the verge of a conflagration like the present because Austria has resisted any intelligent solution of the Balkan question. Now, if the war goes as we all hope and believe it will go, the question will be settled. The Turk, who has no business in Europe, because he is incapable of sharing European ideas, will be driven out of Europe. Russia will have Constantinople, essential to her as giving her that free entrance to the Mediterranean which is her right. England will take the Persian Gulf and make the Euphrates Valley as prosperous as the Nile Valley, and Egypt also will be managed in a less anomalous fashion. Servia will have her sea-board on the Adriatic. Bulgaria, if she is not seduced into sharing the suicide of Turkey, will have her port on the Ægean. Greece will get back all the islands in which the races of ancient Greece, who taught the world its civilization, have remained so much purer than in Athens itself. Rumania will annex all the Rumanian districts which lie outside of its present borders, and Italy, if she joins the Powers of the Triple Entente, will not only get back the Italian provinces which still remain under the rule of Austria, but will have a footing on the Balkan Peninsula, lower down, which will enable her to fulfil her natural mission of being the channel of commerce and civilization for all the Balkan nations.

For many years this has been the natural solution of the Eastern Question, but Austria has stood in the way—Austria, which just as naturally pictured herself overrunning the Balkan Peninsula, and finding her way down to the great southern port of Salonika. Germany backed up Austria, in the hope perhaps that Austria, containing so many people of German nationality, would one day come into the German Empire. The difficulty was that the Balkan Peninsula was all in Slav hands or a natural inheritance for the Slavs. Without conquering Russia, the Austrian dreams were unrealizable, and rather than allow the Balkan Slavs to fulfil their mission, Austria preferred to perpetuate a state of wars and rumours of wars. Turkey's suicidal entrance into the arena has rendered a settlement possible.

If Frederick had foreseen this he would doubtless have left us his warnings on the subject. He was free enough with his warnings as to the trouble which might ensue from the restless energy of the Emperor Joseph the Austrian.

It would not be right for me to conclude this brief survey of Treitschke's judgment on Frederick without quoting the intelligent anticipation of the Dane Bernstorff, writing to Choiseul, one of the trifling Frenchmen whose employment by Louis XV rendered Frederick's task so much easier in his wars with France. "Everything which you undertake to-day to prevent the rise of an entirely military Monarchy in the middle of Germany, whose iron arm will soon crush the minor princes—is all labour wasted!"

DOUGLAS SLADEN.

The Confessions of Frederick the Great

The Confessions of Frederick the Great

The spirit of these Confessions and the principles advocated by Frederick are very closely in line with the teachings of Treitschke and with the national policy championed by Bernhardi.

MORNING THE FIRST

ORIGIN OF OUR FAMILY

IN the times of disorder and confusion, amidst barbarous nations, there was seen to spring up a new arrangement of sovereignties. The governors of different countries shook off the yoke of subjection, and soon became powerful enough to overawe their masters; they obtained privileges, or, to come nearer to the truth, it was with the form of one knee on the ground that they ran away with the substance. Among those daring ones, there were several who laid the foundations of the greatest monarchies; and perhaps, on a fair calculation, even all the emperors, kings, and foreign princes at this very time owe their respective states to them. As for us, we are, most undoubtedly, in that case. I see you blush at this. I forgive you for once; but let me advise you never to play the child so again. Remember, once for all, that, in matter of kingdoms, he catches them that can; and that there is no wrong but in the case of being forced to return them.

The first of our ancestors, who acquired some rights of sovereignty over the country of which he was governor, was Tassillon, of Hohenzollern. The thirteenth of his descendants was Burgrave of Nuremberg; the twenty-fifth of them was Elector of Brandenburg, and the thirty-seventh, King of Prussia. Our family, as well as all the others, has had its Achilles', its Ciceros, its Nestors, its drivellers and its drones, its mothers-in-law, and, without doubt, its women of gallantry. It has also often aggrandized itself by those kinds of right, which are only known to princes at once in luck, and in force enough to exert them; for in the order of our successions, we see those of conveniency, or expectancy, and of protection.

From the time of Tassillon to that of the great Elector, we did little more than vegetate. We could, in the empire, reckon fifty princes in no point inferior to us; and, properly speaking, we were but one of the branches of the great sconce or chandelier of the empire. William the Great, by the splendour of his actions, raised our family into pre-eminence; and at length, in 1701 (the date, you see, is not a very ancient one), vanity placed a crown on the head of my grandfather; and it is to this epoch that we ought to refer our true existence, since it put us into a condition of acting on the footing of kings, and of treating, upon terms of equality, with all the powers of the earth.

Were we to estimate the virtues of our ancestors, we might easily conclude, that it is not to any eminence in them that our family owes its aggrandizement. The greatest part of our princes have been rather remarkable for misconduct; but it was chance and circumstances that have been of service to us. I would even have you to observe, that the first diadem that bound our brows was placed on one of the vainest and lightest of heads, and that head on a body crooked and humpbacked.

And here, I am aware, my dear nephew, that I am leaving you in the dark as to our origin. It has been pretended that that same Count of Hohenzollern was of a great family; but, in truth, few ever appeared in the world so bare of titles. However, at the worst, it is indisputable that we are of an ancient noble extraction: good, good gentlemen, in short; let us stick to that.

THE SITUATION OF MY KINGDOM

As to this point, I am not so well off as I could wish. To convince yourself of which, cast your eyes over the map, and you will see that the greatest part of my territories is dispersed or divided in such a manner, that they cannot mutually assist each other. I have no great rivers that run through my provinces; some border upon them, but few intersect them.[1]

OF THE SOIL OF MY TERRITORIES

A third at least of my dominions lies in waste; another third is in woods, waters, or marshes. The third, which is cultivated, produces nor wine, nor olives, nor mulberry-trees. No fruits nor garden-stuff come to anything, without great care, and very few to the true point of perfection. I have only a few parts in which the wheat and rye have some reputation.

OF THE MANNERS OF THE INHABITANTS

Under this head I have nothing particular or decisive to pronounce, because my kingdom is but a kind of mosaic, made up of various pieces. All that I can, with any certainty, say, is, that, in general, my subjects are hardy and brave, uncurious as to eating, but fond of drinking; tyrants on their estates, and slaves in my service; insipid lovers, and surly husbands; of a wondrously cold, phlegmatic turn, which I take to be at the bottom, rank stupidity; good civilians, little of philosophers, less of poets, and still less of orators;

---

[1] The situation, extent, and soil, of the territories of the great Frederick, have been wonderfully changed of late years; changed upon his own principles, too, as will appear hereafter.—*Note of eighteenth century translator.*

affecting a great plainness in their dress, but imagining themselves dressed in high taste, with a little bag and a great hat, boots up to their waist, a little cane, a very short coat, with a very long waistcoat.

As to the women, they are almost all fat, and special breeders; they have great gentleness, love their domestic employment, and are commonly faithful enough to their husbands. As to the girls, they enjoy the privileges in fashion; to which I have so little objection, that I have, in my memoirs, sought to excuse their weaknesses. I hold it good policy to give those pretty creatures all the ease and freedom that may be, to prevent their learning a horrid practice, by means of which they might amuse themselves without fear of consequences, but which would cause a notable prejudice to the state. Nay, to encourage them the more to population, I take care in my regiments to give the preference to the fruit of their amours; and, if the offspring of an officer, I make him an ensign, and often raise him to higher rank before his turn.

MORNING THE SECOND

ON RELIGION

RELIGION is absolutely necessary in a state. This is a maxim which it would be madness to dispute; and a king must know very little of politics, indeed, that should suffer his subjects to make a bad use of it; but then it would not be very wise in a king to have any religion himself. Mark well, my dear nephew, what I here say to you; there is nothing that tyrannizes more over the head and heart than religion; because it neither agrees with our passions, nor with those great political views which a monarch ought to have. The true religion of a prince is his interest and his glory. He ought, by his royal station, to be dispensed from having any other. He may, indeed, preserve outwardly a fair occasional appearance, for the sake of amusing those who are about him, or who watch his motions and character.

If he fears God, or, to speak as the priests and women do, if he fears hell, like Lewis XIVth,[1] in his old age, he is apt to become timorous, childish, and fit for nothing but to be a capuchin.

---
[1] And, it might be added, ewis XVI.—*Vide* Madame Roland.
—*Footnote of eighteenth century translator.*

If the point is to avail himself of a favourable moment for seizing a province,[1] an army of devils, to defend it, present themselves to his imagination; we are, on that supposition, weak enough to think it an injustice, and we proportion in our conscience, the punishment to the crime. Should it be necessary to make a treaty with other powers, if we remember that we are Christians, we are undone; all would be over with us; we should be constantly bubbles. As to war, it is a trade, in which any the least scruple would spoil everything, and, indeed, what man of honour would ever make war, if he had not the right to make rules that should authorize plunder, fire, and carnage?

I do not, however, mean that one should make a proclamation of impiety and atheism; but it is right to adapt one's thoughts to the rank one occupies. All the popes, who had common sense, have held no principles of religion but what favoured their aggrandizement. It would be the silliest thing imaginable, if a prince were to confine himself to such paltry trifles as were contrived only for the common people. Besides, the best way for a prince to keep fanaticism out of his country is for him to have the most cool indifference for religion. Believe me, dear nephew, that holy mother of ours has her little caprices, like any woman, and is commonly as inconstant. Attach yourself, then, dear nephew, to true philosophy,

[1] Alas, unhappy Poland!—*Footnote of eighteenth century translator.*

which is ever consolatory, luminous, courageous, dispassionate, and inexhaustible as Nature. You will then soon see, that you will not have, in your kingdom, any material dispute about religion; for parties are never formed but on the weakness of princes, or on that of their ministers.

There is one important reflection I would with you make; it is this: your ancestors have, in this matter, conducted their operations with the greatest political dexterity; they introduced a reformation which gave them the air of apostles at the same time that it was filling their purse. Such a revolution was, without doubt, the most reasonable that could ever happen in such a point as this: but, since there is now hardly anything left to be got in that way, and that, in the present position of things, it would be dangerous to tread in their footsteps, it is therefore even best to stick to toleration. Retain well, dear nephew, the principle I am now to inculcate to you: let it be your rule of government, that men are to worship the Divinity in their own way; for, should you appear in the least neglectful of this indulgence, all would be lost and undone in your dominions.

Have you a mind to know why my kingdom is composed of so many sects? I will tell you: in certain provinces the Calvinists are in possession of all the offices and posts; in others, the Lutherans have the same advantage. There are some, where the Catholics are so predominant, that the king can only send there one or two Protestant deputies; and, of all the ignorant and blind fanatics, I dare aver to you that the Papists are the most fiery and the most atrocious. The priests in their senseless religion are untameable wild beasts, that preach up a blind submission to their wills, and exercise a complete despotism. They are assassins, robbers, violators of faith, and inexpressibly ambitious.

Mark but Rome! Observe with what a stupid effrontery she dares arrogate to herself dominion over the princes of the earth! As to the Jews, they are little vagrants, poor devils, that at bottom are not so black as they are painted. Almost everywhere rebuffed, hated, persecuted; they pay with tolerable exactness, those who endure them, and take their revenge by bubbling all the simpletons they can light on.

As our ancestors made themselves in the ninth century, Christians, out of complaisance to the emperors; in the fifteenth, Lutherans, in order to seize the possessions of the church; and Calvinists, in the sixteenth, to please the Dutch, upon the account of the succession of Cleves; I do not see why we should not make ourselves indifferent to all these religions for the sake of maintaining tranquillity in our dominions.

My father had formed an excellent project, but it did not succeed with him. He had engaged the President Laen to compose for him a small treatise on religion, which was to procure a coalition of the three sects into one. The president abused the Pope, hinted that St. Joseph was a soft simpleton, took the dog of St. Roc by the ears, and pulled St. Anthony's pig by the tail; he expressed no faith in the story of the chaste Susannah, he looked on St. Bernard and St. Dominic as courtiers that were refined cheats, and protested against the canonization of St. Francis de Sales for a saint. The eleven thousand virgins met with no more quarter from his credulity than all the saints and martyrs of the Jesuit Loyola.

As to the mysteries, he agreed that no explanation of them should be attempted, but that good sense ought to be put into everything, while he was by no means for being tied up to the mere sound of words. As to the Lutherans, he was for making of them the centre-point of union and of rest. He wanted the Catholics to be, in appearance, somewhat less faithful to the court of Rome; but then he admitted that the Lutherans ought to betray less subtility of argument in their disputes. He insisted, that, on removing certain distinctions out of the way, the sects would find themselves very near to each other. He thought there would be more trouble required to bring the Calvinists to a reconciliation, because they had more pretensions than the Lutherans. In the meanwhile, he proposed one good expedient, which was, not to have any but God for one's confidant, on occasion of taking the communion. He looked on the worship of images as a bait for the common people, but admitted that it was proper for a country to have a tutelar Saint of some kind or other.

As to the Monks, he was for expelling them, because he looked on them as an enemy that always laid the country under heavy contributions. But priests, he allowed them their housekeepers for wives. This scheme made a great noise, because those good ladies, the three mother-churches, thought themselves each respectively aggrieved, and that it was a sacrilege to touch upon the holy mysteries. But if this essay of a project had been relished, there would have been no efforts spared to have effectuated its execution. I have not, my dear nephew, renounced it, and I flatter myself that I shall facilitate to you the execution of it. The great point is, to be useful to the whole of humankind, by rendering all men brothers; and by making it a law to them to live together as friends and relations, by inculcating to them the absolute necessity of living and of dying in commutual peace and concord, and to seek their sole happiness in the social virtues.

When these maxims shall have once taken root in the rising generations, the fruit of it will be the world's forming itself into one numerous family, and the so much celebrated golden age will come up to that state of felicity which I ardently wish to mankind, and which it will then enjoy without adulteration. Now, pray mark what I am doing for this purpose: I use my best endeavours that all the writings in my kingdom, on religion, should breathe the strongest spirit of contempt for all the reformers that ever were, and I never slip any the least occasion of unmasking the ambitious views of the court of Rome, of its priests, and ministers. Thus, little by little, I shall accustom my subjects to think as I do, and shall detach them from all prejudices.

But as it is necessary to have some religious worship, I will, if I live long enough, underhand, bring into play some man of eloquence, who shall preach a new one. At first, I will give myself the air of designing to persecute him: but, little by little, I will declare myself his defender, and will, with warmth, embrace his system. And, if you must know the truth, that system is already made.

Voltaire has composed the preamble to it; he proves the necessity of abandoning everything that has already been said upon religion, because there is no one point of it upon which everyone is agreed. He draws the picture of every chief of a sect with a mildness which bears a kind of resemblance to truth. He has dug up certain curious anecdotes of popes, of bishops, of priests, of ministers, of the other sects, which diffuse a singular gaiety over his work. It is written in a style so close and so rapid as not to leave time for reflection: and, full as this author is of the most subtle art, he has the air of the greatest candour imaginable, while he is advancing the most doubtful principles.

D'Alembert and Maupertuis have formed the groundwork of the plan, and the whole is calculated with such scrupulous exactness, as to tempt one to believe that they had endeavoured to demonstrate it to themselves before they sought to demonstrate it to others. Rousseau has been at work for these four years past, to obviate all objections; and I am anticipating in imagination the pleasure I shall take in mortifying all the ignorant wretches that shall dare to contradict me; for there is an army of prelates and priests, constantly assembled, who are for ever imposing on the populace, which has neither the capacity nor the time to reflect.[1] Thence it comes to pass that, in those countries that swarm with priests, the people are more unhappy and more ignorant than in Protestant countries.

The priests are like soldiers, who do mischief habitually and for amusement. There are already prepared fifty consequences for every object of dispute, and, at least, thirty reflections on each article of the Holy Scriptures. He is even actually taken up with furnishing proofs that everything, at present, preached from thence, is but a fable, that there never was a terrestrial paradise, and that it is degrading God to believe that he made, after his own image, a mere idiot, and his most perfect creature a rank, lewd, jade.

For, in short, adds he, nothing but the length of the serpent's tail could have seduced Eve; and,

[1] So that more countries than one have a swinish multitude.

in that case, it proves there must have been a horrid disorder of her imagination.[1] The Marquis d'Argens and M. Formey have prepared the constitution of a council; I am to preside in it, but without pretending that the Holy Ghost is to give any the least particle of light to me more than to the rest. There shall assist at it but one minister of each sect of religion, and four deputies of every province, two of which to be of the nobility and two of the commons, or third estate. All the other priests, monks and ministers, in general, to be excluded, as being parties concerned in the matter. And that the Holy Ghost may the clearer appear to preside in this assembly, it will be agreed to decide everything honestly according to common sense.

[1] Oh, fie! Frederick!

MORNING THE THIRD

ON JUSTICE

TO our subjects we owe justice, as they owe respect to us.[1] By this, I mean, dear nephew, that we must do justice to all men, and especially to our subjects, when it does not overset our own rights, or wound our own authority; for there ought to be no sort of equality between the right of the monarch and the right of the subject or slave. But we must be firmly impartial and just when the point is to settle a matter of right between one subject, whatever he may be, and another. This is an act which is alone enough to make us adored.

Represent to yourself Charles I brought to the scaffold by that justice which the people implores, and demands with a loud voice. I am born with too much ambition to suffer in my dominion any order that should cramp my authority, and this most certainly is the only reason that obliged me to make a new code of justice. I am very sensible that I have reduced the old dame from her long robes to a jacket and petticoat; but I was afraid

[1] This sentiment need not be quarrelled with, but mark the explanation.

of her sharp sight, as I knew her weight with the people, and knew, withal, that princes of any dexterity might, at the same time that they were satisfying their ambition, make themselves adored.

The greatest part of my subjects really believed that I was moved at the grievances resulting to them from chicanery, or the tedious processes of the law. Alas! I own to you, nay, I sometimes blush to myself for it, that so far from having had such a relief in view, I am actually regretting the little advantages those processes used to procure me; for the taxes on them, and on the stamped papers made use of in them, have suffered a diminution, to the detriment of my revenues, near five hundred thousand livres.

Do not then, my dear nephew, suffer yourself to be dazzled with the word *justice;* it is a word that has different relations, and is susceptible of different constructions. These are the ideas that I annex to it:

Justice is the image of God. Now who can attain to such high perfection? Is it not more reasonable to give up so vain a project as that of an entire possession of her? Review all the kingdoms of the earth, examine and mark whether she is in any two kingdoms administered in the same form. Consult next the principles that rule mankind, and see whether they and Justice agree. What is there, then, so extraordinary in a man's being just after his own way? When I cast my eyes over all the tribunals of my kingdom, I observed an immense army of lawyers, all presumably honest men, and yet violently suspected of not being so.[1]

Every tribunal had its superior; I myself had mine; for even those judgments given by my council were liable to control or opposition. I was not angry at this because it was a custom.[2] But on examining, or rather on observing, chicanery every day gaining ground, and invading the property of my subjects, I was frightened at all

---

[1] "So are we all; all honourable men!"—*Eighteenth century translator's note.*

[2] The men of the law can, in process of time, come to such a pitch, as to be a match for the monarch, to struggle with his power, and even to overset it. Under a weak prince, surrounded with ignorant or avaricious ministers, lawyers will start up, and strengthen themselves with the love of the people, whose cause they affect to embrace; and, little by little, they will accomplish their end of breaking, and levelling in the dust, the idols to which they publicly before burnt incense. Do not let the shrewd management of the parliaments of France be forgotten.

Under the pretext of disburthening from the taxes they are loud for taking off, they exaggerate to the king the public distresses, they paint the state running to its ruin, they give fresh spirit to the boldness of its enemies, destroy the patriotism of the subject, and end with usurping the administration into which they force themselves.

Instead of doing justice to the wretches whom circumstances of oppression compel to apply to them, they drag them at their chariot-wheels, strip them, and send them to die naked on a dung-hill. All the philosophers of Paris loudly exclaim against these open depredations exercised on the weak. The men of the law in that kingdom have been ever depraved, and rapacious of money. Read the Chancellor de l'Hôpital, and you will be convinced of this truth.—*Note by eighteenth century translator.*

the immense bewildering labyrinths in which thousands of my subjects were losing themselves and being devoured alive. But what gave me most disquiet was, the slow, but sure and constant, march of the people of the law, that spirit of liberty inseparable from their principles, and that dextrous management of theirs of preserving their advantages, and of crushing their enemies, with all the appearances of the most austere equity.

I made pass in review before my memory all those acts full of rigour, and often very unaccountable, of the parliaments of England and Paris, and was surprised at some of them being so disgraceful to the majesty of the throne. It was amidst all these reflections that I determined to strike at the foundations of this great power, and it was only by simplifying it as much as I could, that I have reduced it to the point at which I wanted it.

You will, perhaps, be surprised, my dear nephew, that men who have no arms, and who never speak but with respect of the sacred person of the king, should be the only people in his kingdom able to give law to him. It is precisely for these very reasons that it is not difficult for them to check or set bounds to our power. There is no suspecting them of violence, since they always speak to us with the greatest decency, and our subjects are soon captivated and led away in chains by that firm eloquence, which seems never to display itself but for their happiness and our glory.

I have often reflected on the advantages resulting to a kingdom from a body of representatives of the people, which is a depositary of its laws; I am even ready to believe that the crown is the safer on a king's head for its having been given, or for its being preserved, to him by such a body; but that he must be strictly an honest man, and made up of good principles, to permit his actions to stand every day its scrutiny or examination.

When one has ambition, one must renounce that plan; I should never have done anything if I had been cramped. Perhaps I might have obtained the character of a just king, but I should have missed that of a hero.

The limited monarch is oftener exposed to the vicissitudes of fortune than the arbitrary despot; but then the despot must be active, enlightened, and firm. There are more virtues required to give a lustre to a state of despotism than to that of monarchy.

The courtier flatters the monarch, soothes his vices, and deceives him; the slave prostrates himself, but gives him right information. It is, then, of more use to a great man to reign arbitrarily, but more grievous to the people to live under such a government.

MORNING THE FOURTH

ON POLITICS

SINCE it has been agreed among men that to cheat or deceive one's fellow-creatures is a mean and criminal action, there has been sought for, and invented, a term that might soften the appellation of the thing, and the word, wnich undoubtedly has been chosen for the purpose, is *Politics*. Now the word has only been found out in favour of sovereigns, because we cannot quite so decently be called rogues and rascals. But, be that as it may, this is what I think as to *politics*. I understand, then, by this word, dear nephew, that we are ever to try to cheat others. It is the way to have the advantage, or, at least, to be on a footing with the rest of mankind. For you may rest persuaded that all the states of the world run the same career. Now this principle being once settled, never be ashamed of making alliances, and of being yourself the only party that draws advantage from them. Do not commit that stupid fault of not abandoning them whenever it is your interest so to do; and especially maintain vigorously this maxim, that stripping your neighbours is only to take away from them the means of doing you a mischief.

It is politics, properly speaking, that found kingdoms and preserve them; so that, dear nephew, it is fit that you understand them thoroughly, and conceive them in their clearest light. For this purpose, I shall make two divisions of them to you, the one POLITICS of the STATE, and the other PRIVATE POLITICS; the first turns on the great interests of the kingdom; the other on the particular interests of the king, and of this we shall first treat.

ON PRIVATE POLITICS

A prince ought never to present to view but the fairest aspect of character, and this is a point to which you must pay a very serious attention. When I was only prince royal, I had very little of a military turn; I loved my ease and the pleasures of the table, and, as to love, I made it on all sides.

When I came to be king, I appeared the soldier, the philosopher, the poet; I lay upon straw, I ate ammunition-bread at the head of my camp; I drank very little before my subjects, and appeared to have a contempt for women.

As for my personal conduct, it is this: in my journeys I always go without a guard, and travel night and day; my train is far from numerous, but well chosen. My carriage is plain, but then it is hung upon special easy springs, and I sleep in it as well as in my bed.

I seem to have no nicety about my eating and drinking. A lacquey, a cook, a confectioner, are all the menials I have for providing my table. I order my own dinner myself, and it is not what I acquit myself the worst of, as I know the country; and whatever I call for, of wild game, of fish, or butcher's meat, it is always sure to be of the best produce of the land.

When I come to a place of inhabitants, I have always a fatigued air, and show myself to the people in a very shabby surtout and a wig ill combed.

These are trifles, but trifles that often make a marvellous impression. I give audience to the whole universe, except to priests, ministers of the Church, and monks; as those gentry are used to speak so as to be heard at a distance, I hear them from my window; a page receives them, and makes my compliments to them at the door. In everything I say, I affect the air of thinking of nothing but the happiness of my subjects; I ask questions of the nobility, of citizens, of mechanics, and enter with them into the minutest particulars.

You have, my dear nephew, heard, as well as myself, the flattering discourse of those good kinds of people. You cannot forget him that said, that I must be an extraordinary good king, who could put myself to so much fatigue after having carried on so long a war. You may also remember him, who pities me from his heart, on observing the bad surtout I had on, and the small dishes that were served on my table. The poor man did not know that I had a very good coat underneath, and could not imagine it possible to dine anything like well without a ham and a whole shoulder of veal on the table.

At a review of my troops, before a regiment is to pass muster, I take care to read over the names of all its officers and sergeants, and I retain three or four of them, with the names of the companies to which they belong. I procure an exact information of the petty abuses which may have been committed by my captains, and I allow the soldiers liberty of complaining.

The hour of the review being come, I set out from wherever I am. Presently the mob gets round me; nor do I suffer it to be kept off, but chat by the way with the first person that is nearest me, or that can make the most reasonable answer. As soon as I am come to the regiment, I see that the exercise be without too much trouble, and rather with ease, performed throughout all the ranks, and I speak to all the captains. When I am over-against those whose names I have retained, I speak to them freely, as likewise to all the lieutenants and sergeants: this gives me a wonderful fine air of memory and reflection.

You saw, dear nephew, in what manner I mortified the major who used to furnish his company with shirts too short; I used him so ill, that one of the soldiers had the impudence, by way of shewing the scanty measure, to pull his shirt out of his breeches.

If a regiment does not acquit itself of the exercise to my satisfaction, I have a kind of punishment for it that is not amiss; I order it to perform the exercise for thirteen days longer than usual, and ask none of the officers to my table. If the manœuvres are well executed, I have all the captains to dine with me, and even some of the lieutenants.

By means, then, of the reviews being conducted in this manner, I come at a perfect knowledge of my troops; and when I find any officer that answers me with firmness, intelligence, and clearness, I set him down in my list for making use of his service on proper occasions.

Hitherto it has been believed by the world that it is the stark love and kindness I bear to my subjects that engages me to visit my dominions as often as I possibly can. I like to leave that same world in quiet possession of that idea; but there enters very little of the reality of such a motive into that trouble I give myself; the truth is, that I am obliged to it, and this is the reason.

My kingdom is despotic, consequently I, who am the possessor of it, am alone in charge of it. If I did not make, at times, a tour of inspection through my dominions, my governors would put themselves in my place, and would, little by little, divest themselves of their principles of obedience, and adopt in their stead those of independence.

Besides, as my orders cannot be other than stern and absolute, those who represent me would usurp the same tone of tyranny. Whereas, by visiting my kingdom from time to time, I am enabled to take cognizance of all the abuses that may have been committed of the powers intrusted by me, and to keep within the bounds of their duty such as might otherwise take it into their head to transgress them.

Add to these reasons, that of making my subjects believe, that I come familiarly among them purely to receive their complaints, and to redress their grievances.

ON LITERATURE

I have done everything in my power to acquire a reputation in literature, and, in that, have been more successful than Cardinal Richelieu, for, thank God, I pass for an author; but, between you and me, and not to let it go any farther, they are a damned set of people, those they call wits. They are insupportable for their vanity; insolent, despising the great, and yet fond of greatness: tyrants in their opinions, implacable enemies, inconstant friends, difficult to live with, and often flatterers and satirists in the same day. And yet, for all this, they are necessary beings to a prince who would reign despotically, and who loves glory. They are the dispensers of the honours of celebrity; without them, there is no acquiring a solid reputation. They must, then, be caressed from our need of them, and recompensed from good policy.

As this is a profession, or call it, if you will, a trade, that takes us off from the occupations worthy of the majesty of the throne, I never compose but when I have nothing better to do; and to give myself the more ease in it, I keep at my court some wits, who take care to put my ideas into order.

You have seen with what distinction I treated Monsieur D'Alembert in his last visit here; I always set him at my table, and did nothing but praise him. You even seemed surprised at the great respect I shewed this author; but you do not know, perhaps, that this philosopher is listened to at Paris like an oracle; that he talks of nothing else there but of my talents and my virtues; and that he maintains everywhere that I fulfil the character of a true hero and of a great king.

Besides, there is a sort of pleasure to me, in hearing myself praised with wit and delicacy; and, to deal sincerely with you, I am far from being insensible to panegyric. I cannot dissemble to myself, that all my actions are not clearly praiseworthy; but D'Alembert is so good-natured, that, when he sits by me, he never opens his mouth but to say obliging things to me.

Voltaire was not of so pliable a character; accordingly I drove him from my court, of which I made a merit to Maupertuis, though the true reason at bottom was, that I stood in fear of him, because I was not sure that I could always humour his avarice, and knew perfectly well, that half-a-crown less than he expected would draw on me two thousand scratches from his satirical claws.

Besides, everything well considered, and after having taken the advice of my academy, it was a clearly decided point that it was impossible for two wits to breathe the same air.

I was forgetting to tell you, that in the midst of my greatest straits and disasters, I took care that the wits should have their pensions duly paid them. These philosophers exclaim against war as the most execrable of all madnesses the moment that it touches their pocket.

CONDUCT IN THE SMALLER MATTERS OF LIFE

Have you a mind to satisfy all the world at a very little cost? This is the secret. Let all your subjects have leave to apply to yourself directly by writing, or in personal audience; and, according as you admit of either of these, answer or hear what they have to say. But this is the style you are to employ:

"*If what you tell me be true, I will do you justice; but you may also lay your account with the zeal I have for punishing calumny and falsity. I am your king, F——ck.*"

If they complain, in person, to you, hear them with attention, or at least with an air that may make them think you have it. Let your answer especially be firm and laconic. Two letters, or two verbal answers, in such a style, will save you from the importunity of many complaints, and will give you among your own subjects, and more yet in foreign courts, such an air of simplicity, and of descending into particulars, as in point of character makes the fortune of kings.

I am well assured, dear nephew, that on the credit of two letters of this kind, actually extant in those countries which the French took in 1757, I passed among them for a king the most popular, the most plain-dealing, and the most equitable, that ever was or could be.

AS TO DRESS

If my grandfather had lived twenty years more, we should have been an undone people, for his birthday would have devoured the kingdom. I never wear any coat but my uniform. The military imagine that this proceeds from the regard I have for their profession; but in fact it is to make my example enforce my preachments of simplicity of dress. My father was right in his notion of bringing in the blue for birthdays.

Those who are not rich, and would appear well dressed, would do well to avoid the half-lace. One should leave embroidery, and the tawdry daubings of gold and silver, to those idle, effeminate princes who live in the midst of nothing but pleasures, balls, and debauchery. There is a necessity for the frivolous to study every day some new fanciful taste in dress, that they may please the ladies, which they make their sole occupation.

AS TO PLEASURES

Love is a little deity that spares no one. When one resists those darts he lets fly at us in a fair way, he takes another turn; so that I would not wish you to have the vanity of making head against him. One way or other he is sure of you. Though I have not to complain of the trick he has played me, I would not advise you to follow my example. It might come in time to have very bad consequences; for, by degrees, your governors and officers would, in their choice of recruits, consult more their own pleasures than the honour of your service, and your army might come at length to be like the regiment of your uncle Henry.

I should have liked hunting well enough, but the accompt-expenses of my grandfather's grand huntsman corrected me of that inclination.

My father has told me a hundred times, that there were but two kings in Europe rich enough to keep buck-hounds, because it is indecent for a crowned head to hunt with no more state than a private gentleman.

Nature has given me self-indulgent-enough dispositions. I love good eating, good wines, coffee, and even spirituous cordials, and yet my subjects believe me the most abstemious king in the universe. When I eat in public, it is my German cook that dresses my dinner; but when I am snug in my little private apartments, I have a French cook who does his best to humour my palate, which, I must confess, is rather of the nicest. Philosophers may say what they will, with all their lessons, but the pleasures of the senses very well deserve that we should spare them a couple of hours a day; for, in fact, what would our existence be without them?

I could take a pleasure in play, but I cannot bring myself to a habit of enduring to lose. Besides, play is the looking-glass of the soul; and this does not at all do for me, for I do not much care that anyone should look into mine.

I love theatrical entertainments extremely, and especially music; but I find the Opera cursedly dear, and the pleasure I take in hearing a fine voice or a good violin would be much more lively and pure if it did not cost me so much money.

As no one can be imposed upon as to this expense, I have used my best endeavours to persuade that it was useful and even necessary; but I never could get the old generals to come into the opinion, that an eunuch or a virtuoso ought to have the same pay as they.

I will now give up to you the knowledge of man, though at his expense. Believe me, he is always delivered up to his passions; vanity is at the bottom of all his thirst after glory, and his virtues are all founded on his self-interest and ambition. Have you a mind to pass for a hero? Make boldly your approaches to crimes. Would you like to be thought virtuous? Learn to appear artfully what you are not.

MORNING THE FIFTH

ON POLITICS OF THE STATE

THESE politics may be reduced to three heads, or principles. The first, self-preservation, and aggrandizement, according to circumstances. Second, alliances never to be made but for one's own advantage. And the third, to make one's self respected and feared in the most difficult times.

PRINCIPLE THE FIRST

OF SELF-PRESERVATION AND AGGRANDIZEMENT

On my ascending to the throne, I visited the coffers of my father. His great economy, I found, had put me in a condition of conceiving great projects. Soon afterwards I made a review of my troops, and fine ones they appeared to me: upon which I returned to my coffers, and took out of them wherewith to double my military force.

As I had then just rendered my power twice as great as it was before, it was natural for me not to be contented with only preserving what I had, so that I was quickly determined to avail myself of the first opportunity that should offer. In the meanwhile I exercised my troops, and used my

Confessions of Frederick the Great 67

best endeavours to draw the eyes of all Europe on my *manœuvres;* I renewed them every year, in order to appear more and more master of the art of war; and at length I obtained my wish of procuring a general attention.

I turned the head of all the powers, and all the world gave themselves up for lost, if their military did not move head, legs, and arms, *à la mode* of the Prussian exercise. All my soldiers and my officers took it into their heads that they were twice the men they were before on seeing they were everywhere aped.

When my troops had thus acquired an advantage over all the others, I had nothing to do but to examine what pretensions it was possible for me to form upon different provinces. Four different points offered themselves to my view: *Silesia, Polish Prussia, Dutch Gueldre and Swedish Pomerania.*

I fixed, however, on *Silesia,* both because that object deserved my attention more than all the others put together, and because the circumstances were more favourable to me.

I left to time the care of the execution of my projects on the other points. I will not here enter on a demonstration to you of the validity of my pretensions on Silesia, I took care to have it established by my orators. The empress-queen opposed hers to them, and the cause was pleaded and decided by great guns, small arms, and sabres. But let me return to those favourable circumstances I intimated: thus it was that they presented themselves. France wanted to take the empire out of the hands of the House of Austria:—there was nothing I wished for more. France also had a mind to form in Italy a state for the Infant:—this too I liked, because it could not be done but at the expense of the empress-queen. In short, France had conceived the noble project of marching to the gates of Vienna:—that was the very point I waited for, that I might seize upon Silesia.

Be then, my dear nephew, provided of money; wait for circumstances; and be assured of not barely preserving your dominions, but of aggrandizing them. There are certain small politicians who pretend, that, when a state is arrived at a certain point, it ought not to think of aggrandizement, because the system of the balance of power has limited each state to a certain fixed extent.

I remember that the ambition of Lewis XIVth had like to have cost France dear, and I am not insensible of all the disquiet that mine has given me: I know, also, that France, in the midst of her greatest disasters, disposed of a crown, and preserved the provinces she had conquered; and you may, as to myself, see, that, amidst all the storm that threatened me, I have lost nothing; so that everything depends on the circumstances of the times, and on the courage of him that takes and holds.

You cannot, my dear nephew, conceive how important it is for a king and a state to go often out of the common road; it is only by the marvellous that one can strike an awe into others, or get a great name.

The Balance is a word that has subdued the whole world, by the light in which it was considered of its securing a constant possession; and yet, in truth, this same Balance is no more than a bare word, an empty sound; for Europe is a family in which there are too many bad brokers and quarrelsome relations.

I go farther yet, dear nephew: it is by the contempt of this system that one must come at anything that is great. Behold the English, they have put the sea in chains; that fierce unruly element no longer dares carry any vessels but with their permission.

From all this, it results, that it is good policy to be always attempting something, and to be perfectly persuaded that we have a right to everything that suits us.

You must only take care not to make, with too much vanity, too open a proclamation of such pretensions; and especially to maintain at your court two or three persons of eloquence, and leave it in charge with them to justify you.

PRINCIPLE THE SECOND

ON ALLIANCES

To form alliances for one's advantage is a great maxim of state, and there are no powers that can answer to themselves a neglect of it. Thence, by clear inference, it follows, that you should break an alliance as soon as ever it becomes prejudicial to you.

In my first war with the Queen of Hungary, I abandoned France at Prague, because I got Silesia by the bargain. If I had escorted the French safe to Vienna, they would never have given me so much. Some years after I renewed with them, because I had a mind to attempt the conquest of Bohemia, and thought it best to keep measures with this power, against I might have occasion for its assistance. Since that time I have neglected that nation, in order to come in with another that offered me more.

When Prussia, dear nephew, shall have made her fortune, it will be time enough for her to give herself an air of fidelity to engagements and of constancy; an air, which, at the most, becomes none but great states or little sovereigns. I have already, dear nephew, told you that politics and villainy are almost synonymous terms, and I told you the truth. And yet you will, on this head, find some people who have formed to themselves certain systems of probity; so that you may hazard anything by means of your ambassadors. I have found some that have served me in very delicate occasions, and who, to come at a mystery, would have rummaged or picked the pockets of a king.

Let your choice fall especially on those who have

the talent of expressing themselves in vague, indefinite, terms, or in squinting and perplexed phrases. You would not do amiss to have at your devotion some political physicians and locksmiths; they may sometimes be of great use to you. I know, by experience, all the advantages that may be gained by their means.

PRINCIPLE THE THIRD

OF INSPIRING RESPECT AND FEAR

To make one's self respected and feared by one's neighbours is the very summit of high policy. This end is to be achieved by two means:—the first, is to have a real force and effectual resources; —the second, is to make the most of the strength one has.—Now we are not within the first case, and that is the reason of my having neglected nothing that might make me shine in the second.

There are powers who imagine that an embassy should always be sent with great splendour, and cut a great figure. Monsieur de Richelieu, however, only served at Vienna to put the French into a ridiculous light; for the Austrians concluded, that the whole nation smelt as strong of musk and amber as he that represented it.

As for me, I rather hold that it is more by the noble manner in which an ambassador makes his master speak, than by the parade of his equipages or retinue, that he gains a true or valuable respect;

—it is for this reason that I propose never more to employ ambassadors, but only envoys. Besides, the first of these characters is too difficult to fill suitably, as it requires a man of great note or distinction, very rich, and who understands politics perfectly; whereas, with this last advantage only, an envoy may serve sufficiently for the purpose.

By adopting this system, you will every year save a considerable sum, and your business will be as well done. There are, however, some occasions, in which it is necessary to show away with some magnificence; as, for example, when you come to a rupture with a court, or make an alliance, or for a nuptial ceremony. But these embassies must be ever considered as extraordinary.

Never ask faintly, but seem rather to demand. If you have any cause of discontent given you, reserve your revenge for the moment in which you may obtain the most complete satisfaction, but especially do not stand in fear of reprisals; your glory will not suffer for it, it will only be so much the worse for those of your subjects on whom the damage may fall. It must, then, be your great aim that all your neighbours should be persuaded that you fear nothing, and that nothing can astonish you.

Endeavour, above all things, to pass with them for one of a dangerous cast of mind, who knows no other principles but those that lead to military fame. Manage so that they may be fully convinced that you would sooner lose two kingdoms

Frederick the Great

than not play a part that may transmit you to posterity. As these sentiments are those of a soul above the common order, they strike, they confound, the greatest part of mankind; and it is this that, in truth, constitutes in the world the greatest monarchs.

When a stranger comes to your court, overwhelm him with civilities, and especially try to have him always near you; this will be the best way to keep concealed from him the defects of your government.

If he is a military man, let the exercise of your regiments be performed before him, and let it be yourself that commands them. If he is a wit who has composed a work, let him see it lying on your table, and talk to him of his talents. If he is in a mercantile life, listen to him with affability, caress him, and try to fix him in your country.

MORNING THE SIXTH

MILITARY

A CELEBRATED author has compared the military to mastiffs which ought to be chained up carefully, and ought not to be loosed except when necessary. The comparison is rather strained, but, for all that, it will serve you, not as a maxim, but as a warning.

You have been able to learn in the two campaigns which you have made with me the spirit of officer and soldier, and you have been able to perceive that in general they are veritable machines, with no other forward movement than that which you give them.

You persuade these troops that they are superior to those whom you oppose to them; a mere nothing makes them believe that they are weaker; it is, however, these nothings which make the glory or disgrace of a general.

Therefore apply yourself to get a good knowledge of the causes which produce them. I go further, and say that it is the nothings which create the enthusiasm, and if once you can confer it on your army, you can count on victory.

I will not recall here that which you will have

noticed in history, but remember only the Russians, and you will acknowledge that only inspired beasts could stand being slaughtered like them.

My kingdom, by its nature, is military, and, shortly speaking, it is only by its assistance that you can hope to sustain and aggrandize yourself. It is necessary, therefore, that your attention should always be fixed on this. But you must take care that the military should not perceive that they are your only resource. When I took over the reins of Government, I looked into this to the bottom, and corrected it; but it was not without much trouble that I arrived at the goal of my design, for your officer does not readily bend to new regulations, above all when it touches his own personal interest. You can judge of this by two examples.

The captains had each a district (canton) for recruiting. Every male infant who was born in that canton was by right his captain's soldier, and was registered as such from the cradle.

It is true that his father could buy him out, but if that captain happened to die, the buying out was annulled, and the infant became once more by right the soldier of the new captain.

You understand well what authority this captain exercised in this unhappy canton; he became its tyrant.

During the lifetime of my father I was several times offended with this, and when I became the Master, I resolved to abolish such an oppression.

However, you must not offend the old soldiers who know nothing but their routine, above all, when it is advantageous to them.

I amassed proofs, therefore, and soon had more than I wanted. They showed me, among others, that Captain Colan, of the Regiment of Opo (infantry), had drawn from his canton in ten years more than fifty thousand crowns, and they made me see that there was in general no captain who did not derive a revenue of two thousand crowns from the country under him.

Accordingly, I reformed this abuse, but, believe me, most of my generals wished to prove to me that it was a great advantage for me, because by it one was surer of training a soldier as one wished, and one knew his character from his infancy. And, in fine, a thousand other like stupidities.

Believe me, also, that in spite of the most absolute orders, there were majors who always went this way, and that I was obliged to cashier two or three who would not submit.

My father had a passion for tall men: he adored the captains who got most of them: it was enough for a soldier to be six feet two or three inches for him to be allowed to do anything, and a captain who had twenty of this height was sure to enjoy the good graces of the King. From this sprang a lax and very variable discipline, and a service of parade.

As I did not have the same taste, I did not make any exceptions. I wished the tall to be punished in the same way as the short: I only took into consideration the goodness of the soldier, and not his height. This conduct displeased my officers very much, as well as my giants. The former were alarmed by the desertions, which, in truth, were then considerable. Because the great statures were not respected, they had even the effrontery to tell me that a man of six feet two or three inches deserved consideration, and ought not to be subjected to ordinary discipline. I asked them the reason for it: they did not know what to reply: in consequence of which the difference soon ceased to exist.

You can see by these two examples how much the particular interest is reckoned above the general interest, and at the same time the attention which you ought to pay to the representations of the military, when you touch their pockets.

You must take great care, my dear nephew, not to confuse the word discipline: it is a word which can only draw its signification from the spirit of the faculties and the situation in the state of which you employ it. It means that each state ought to have its special discipline, and it is mad for it to wish to adopt that of its neighbour. I am going to make you understand this by my own position.

A very wise regulation made by my father was the foundation of our modern discipline. Listen to it well. Following this rule each captain is obliged to have two thirds of his company foreigners. But to make these foreigners feel more like citizens, and to make their lot, which is really rather an unhappy one, since they have no hope of seeing it finish, pleasanter, we have thought that we ought to bestow upon these poor people that air of freedom and authority over the rest of mankind which they like to assume.

And in consequence we do not pay much attention to the little tricks which they play in the garrisons: we grant them in this respect a sort of independence which makes them forget their misfortunes: they think themselves somebodies, and this idea alone saves them from despair.

This discipline does not agree badly with my subjects who are soldiers: by this means they contract an advantageous idea of their trade, and little by little they accustom themselves to regard it as a profession.

We believe that discipline alone constitutes a soldier. We are mistaken; it is oftener the tone which we give him: I have proved this in my recent wars, where I had not already done so in my former wars.

The armies of the Empire and Sweden filled my ranks every day, and these men had no sooner donned my uniform than they were Prussians, and in the first encounter one could only recognize them by their singular valour. Discipline itself must be subordinate to such circumstances, it could not be so good if it was always equal.

When I commenced war my troops recognized

me, and most of my soldiers loved me, because I paid them, fed them and entertained them well. At the same time, I was severe, and expected my orders to be executed with the utmost rigour; I passed nothing, especially when they were under arms.

After two campaigns I changed this severity for pleasantness. I had nothing but deserters for recruiting my army. I could neither pay them nor feed them nor maintain them well. I was obliged to pay them in debased money. It was my belief that I ought to attach them to myself by some means at some point. I tried to inspire them with an air of jollity, and relaxed my hand on marauding: I pretended not to mind when they took the roof off a house to make their fires, and I spared no effort to make them think well of themselves; I shut my eyes to many small negligences in their service; I only punished them lightly. When a regiment played up a little too much, I sent it to Saxony, and my brother Henry, who was in the secret, put matters on a proper footing, because his army was only engaged in observation.

Your principal object, my dear nephew, ought to be to create good officers and good generals, so you ought to make a plan of discipline, and still more, of conduct for them. Behold what I have done up to the present in this line.

In time of peace as well as in time of war, I go into the smallest details with them. Every officer is under the belief that he is known to me personally, and there is no general with whom I am not in relation. Although they play the chief rôle in my dominions, they are no more than the head slaves. An officer and a general cannot leave his post without proper permission; and if either did leave it without my permission, it is a hanging matter. By this means, when I have a valuable man, I keep him always.

The most fortunate officers have three years of misery and humiliation to go through (at the beginning of their careers). Of misery because they have wretched appointments, and of humiliation because the discipline is terrible. To recompense them, I make their lot very honourable when they come to the higher ranks. But, even then, they have no chance of retiring.

In the present war I have not named one of them to a command, to a provincial governorship or a headquarters' appointment which has fallen vacant. To give my officers ambition, I give them great distinction for brilliant performances. In the battle of Rosbach I embraced a cavalry major in the middle of the action, and I conferred the Order of True Merit on an officer in the field. At Dresden I sent my carriage for the lieutenant in the Guards who had been wounded after having attacked the same entrenchment four times. And I gave him his company.

To inspire them with a contempt for death, I had the famous ode of General Keith recited to them, and I had the *libre avôitre* preached to them all through the war.

While I had the money I paid them well, and when my resources were diminished, I debased the coinage. But I overlooked some of the little tricks which they played upon their hosts, when times became harder, and I let them be witnesses of my misfortunes; I gave them the idea that their constancy was the only thing which could rescue us from our embarrassments, which have really been very lamentable in the latest campaigns.

I do not know how I succeeded in reducing to the greatest exactitude in the army those who were regular bandits, and who had an air of the greatest arrogance. I appeared to inspire them with a way of thinking to suit the circumstances. They were Arabs who crushed the country but won the battles.

The same spirit animated, more or less, the general officers: I closed my eyes to all the oppressions which they committed; they worked for me in working for themselves. In which way it was necessary that we should live together. Everyone told me that Major Keller, the Commandant at Leipzig, was feathering his nest. I knew it well, but other people did not know that he was worth millions a year to me.

As one gets accustomed little by little to his ease, and as one learns more and more how to live well, I had generals who were not too anxious to seek glory in the heat of the fray. I knew them well, and I explained to them generally the necessity of showing themselves well and confronting the greatest dangers. I preached by shewing them the way, and made two or three examples. From this moment everybody was dauntless.

When you give a command, leave nothing to be brought home by your generals: confer an air of superiority always on the Profession of Arms. But always attribute to your generals the disaster of a battle, or the disastrous result of a campaign.

You have seen how I punished Le Kizel[1] and Fink[2] for the surrender at Maxin, Zartroit[3] for the surrender at Schweidnitz, and Roulé[4] for having advised the surrender of the citadel of Gratz.[5] In point of fact, none of these were their fault: they were mine.

You are not, my dear nephew, in a position to exercise a very rigorous discipline, and you are obliged to avoid increasing the yoke; real men are rare in your dominions, and foreigners cost too much for you to take them. You need not alter the administration of justice in your regiments, but you should make the death penalty very rare. Make your surgeons observe the same principles as I have impressed upon them, with regard to the arms and legs of your soldiers and your officers.

Do not demand from a subaltern anything more than good routine, because you have no need for

---

[1] A misspelling which cannot be identified. [2] Should be FINCK. [3] Should be ZASTROW. [4] Should be FOUQUET. [5] Should be GLATZ.

Frederick the Great

him to know anything more. But demand from a higher officer genius and theory; and, above all, make a point of not confusing details with great principles, and especially make a great difference between a good quartermaster and a great general, because you can be one without being the other.

I am now coming to the point of my theories about common soldiers and subaltern officers. It is a question now of laying before your eyes the ideas I have maintained in my recent campaigns.

When I saw that France, the Queen of Hungary (Maria Theresa) and Russia were against me, I abandoned half my dominions in order to concentrate and put myself in a condition to be able to invade Saxony.

This manœuvre was universally attributed to a fine stroke of politics. It was really due to necessity, because I should none the less have lost all my dominions if I have been crushed in defending them.

Before the commencement of the war I laid down a system which I have never abandoned: I have always hung on with the greatest obstinacy to part of Saxony: and though I have been surrounded on all sides, I have never been willing to retire from this country, and I was well advised, for I should have been lost without power of recovery.

I know well that it is considered extraordinary that I have allowed Berlin to be laid under contribution twice, and that all the towns in my kingdom, except five or six, have been taken. But everything has been given back to me, as the price of retiring from Saxony.

If you were to consult my subjects at the present moment, I believe that you would find that the enthusiasm is a little dwindled. I am persuaded myself that they have long ago begun to reckon the obligations of a prince to his subjects.

I had made the late war as a pupil. Marshal d'Anhalt[1] and Marshal de Schwerin gave battle; I only figured in the battles. In this campaign my *amour propre* had desired to play the leading part. I had need of Marshal Schwerin; I felt that he was necessary; but I was jealous of his glory. It is certain that if he had not been killed, I should have been ungrateful.

People pay me, my dear nephew, a little more honour than I deserve. For since his death I have made several bad mistakes. I lost the battle of Kollin and raised the siege of Prague quite unnecessarily; I made a false move when I arrived in Moravia, and Marshal Daun, like a good General, had secured Olmütz before he left Vienna.

At Maxin I lost fifteen thousand men by pigheadedness, and ignorance, because I did not see that Marshal Daun had advanced with his army.

General Laudon profited by a false move which I made to take me in the flank at Schweidnitz; I let him crush poor Fouquet before Glatz.

I should have lost the battle of Torgau if Mar-

[1] Leopold of Anhalt-Dessau—the old Dessauer.

shal Daun had not been wounded, and the Russians have beaten me three times out of four; I have never been able to retake Dresden; and I have been fifty-nine days in the open trenches before Schweidnitz.

For all that, I am a general, and no one could dispute that I have great abilities, for, if I have lost battles, I have won them also, and I have made retreats which have won me infinite honour; I have discovered admirable expedients for extricating myself from the most cruel embarrassments.

But, my dear nephew, what has saved me is my desperateness and my vanity. I have preferred to be buried under the ruins of my kingdom to yielding, and it is my obstinacy which has worn everyone out. A man can try this once, but if he is wise he does not expose himself to it a second time.

At present, while I am in cold blood, I see all my glory vanishing in smoke; I have made a noise, but what have I gained? Nothing! On the contrary, I have lost much since the election of the King of the Romans has taken place.

You know the ambition of our house, and I assure you that I shall die of grief if I do not make the Empire pass to some Protestant Prince.

But what afflicts me most is the state of affairs in my own dominions. When I compare the situation of my kingdom in '56 with its situation today, I am confounded. I must lay it before you in order that, in advance, you may come to the resolution of sacrificing everything to re-establish it.

Since '56 I have lost by fighting more than three hundred thousand men. The population is decreased by more than one third, the number of horses and other animals by more than a half; the treasure accumulated by my father has been consumed, and my coinage is debased by one tenth. All the Provinces pay twice as heavily as they did in '56, by the interest of the money which they have been obliged to borrow for the contributions of which it is impossible for me to keep count.

I have no commerce outside of my kingdom, because my money loses too much in exchange abroad, and the bankruptcy of M. Donenville has made me lose all my credit.

The majority of my magazines are empty, my artillery is very bad, and I have very few munitions of war left; it is this which determines me to demolish most of my fortifications: for I am no longer in a condition to put the places which I have abandoned in a state of defence.

Otherwise, in a moment, if I were to come to have war, it would be absolutely impossible for me to guard them.

You see by this that you have no more than one step to take to be ruined, and that would be to undertake a new war, for however glorious it might be for you, it would crush you.

The only way of re-establishing yourself is to make an alliance with England to pay you heavy subsidies to conduct the campaign, and to keep within your borders as long as possible.

It would not be a question of waging an offensive war; you would no longer be in a condition to reassemble large armies, because you could not supply them either with provisions or with munitions of war. It would only, therefore, be in the last extremity that you ought to advance.

In what situation would you find yourself, if your dominions were once more the prey of the enemy? How would your dominions pay in the future the interest on the contributions they had borrowed? To what extent would your people not suffer, and how far would the deficiency in animals not go?

As for me, I cannot resist the sad ideas which this picture presents to me. I know the reputation which I bear throughout Europe, of loving war, and I confess that it is my passion, but I know its calamities, and I yield to the evidence. It is not possible to do this, because I should risk the entire ruin of my dominions.

I pretend to be wicked, but I do it to impose on others. One is not lucky twice, or, to put it better, fortune becomes greedy when one demands too much. She would certainly not be sufficiently generous to rescue our house a second time from the abyss in which it found itself in '57 and '61.

In '57, in the month of October, the French were at the gates of Magdeburg; the Austrians had Schweidnitz and Breslau, the Russians had all Prussia, and part of Brandenburg, and the Swedes had nearly all Pomerania. Berlin had been made to pay a ransom, and all my allies were prisoners.

Rossbach saved me at the edge of the precipice, and the affair of Breslau removed me further back from it for a year.

In '58 the Russians had my kingdom in their hands for three days: if I had unluckily yielded, I should have been lost irretrievably.

At the end of '61, in the month of November, Colberg being taken, the Russians were masters of the road to Berlin; the Austrians with the possession of Schweidnitz and Glatz could dispose of Silesia; the French, with the occupation of Hesse, shut me in on the side of Franconia; and Marshal Daun had more than half of Saxony; I scarcely had enough room for quartering my troops.

Add to this situation the lack of money and clothing for my troops, and, what is worse, the lack of provisions. At this critical moment the Empress of Russia came to die.[1] If it had been I who had frightened her into it, the thing could not have happened more opportunely.

At the peace, like everyone, I made reforms, but I did not follow the order of seniority. I dismissed all the officers whom I suspected of being bad—I have already told you that I had over-

---

[1] Peter III, an admirer of Frederick's, recalled the Russian army directly the Empress Elizabeth died.

looked many things while campaigning, but I had recorded on my tablets all their bad actions, and when I no longer had any need of them, I made a crime for them out of that which I had appeared to treat as a petty trouble.

That is, approximately, my way of thinking about the military, and the way in which I have treated it. Now let us talk a little about provisioning armies.

Provisioning is so legitimate, or, rather, so necessary for an army, that it is impossible for the latter to exist without the former, but it is a great question how far one ought to occupy oneself with it.

After mature reflection upon the subject, I have made the following system. I have accustomed my soldiers to do without bread, meat, and wine, and I have allowed them to get their subsistence from the peasants, and I have made no commissariat except when I could not do otherwise.

Since everything was under the Administration, every economy was to my profit. When a regiment arrived at a town, the citizens were obliged to support it for several days. I divided the profits with my soldiers. I gave them three sous and I kept back two, for the bread which they had to take from my magazines.

When an army was advancing and it did without bread for a day, it was so much profit to me. By this arrangement I gained not only sometimes as much as six weeks' provisions in a year, but

I could also risk forced marches, because I need not fear that doing without bread for one or two days would make the army complain.

When you raise the provisioning to a certain level, you cannot move one step without great difficulty, because, before making a move, you have to think of provisioning. Whereas, when the soldier is properly broken in, he himself becomes careful; he does not eat all he has, except when he is sure of being newly provided for, and by this means the general is much less harassed in his operations.

I should never have been able to make the forced marches which I have made, if I had not risked one or two days' provisioning, and if my soldiers had not been persuaded that one can live without bread and meat.

You would not believe, my dear nephew, the advantage which you have when an army is accustomed to this uncertainty. The general need not abuse it, but he can profit by it at moments which are decisive.

In not paying serious attention, except in necessary cases, to the provisioning of the soldier, the air of importance which makes it so expensive is eliminated.

I do not say, however, my dear nephew, that you ought not to regard this matter as one of the essentials, but you ought to know how to profit by the moment for treating it with a sort of indifference.

I do not speak to you of Engineering or Artillery, because, unfortunately, these two branches are still in their infancy with us. We have not sufficient resources to put them on a good footing. You cannot, under any pretext whatever, dispense with your presence at the head of your troops, because two thirds of your soldiers could not be inspired by any other influence except your presence. Since your situation does not permit you to have a well supplied army, you ought to be present to profit by everything. It is following out this principle that as soon as I have entered any country I treat it as if I had conquered it.

I went through Franconia and the Côte de Neuberg; in the contributions[1] which I levied I often took, in place of money, cloth, or shoes, leather, flour, everything, down to peas and beans. Everything is good, my dear nephew, when you have a use to make of it. You ought not to be under any illusion as to the past. Events have made me great, more than my talents or my forces.

The faults of the French founded my glory: the corruption of the Russian generals kept it up for some time, and the divisions between the Austrian generals have nourished it to the end. When you are lucky, the arms which are opposed to you turn to your profit.

Without the armies of the Empire and Sweden

[1] The German army still levies contributions in kind as at Ghent.

I should never have been able to shew mine. It was a real God-send for me. I had thrown such ridicule on these two nations that the soldiers who had any feeling felt themselves dishonoured by serving them.

MORNING THE SEVENTH

CONCERNING FINANCE

NOTHING is so easy, my dear nephew, as to put finance on an honest footing, and nothing renders it tolerable, except the tone which one gives to it. It is in this that I find that my predecessors have conceived very well in creating the Land Courts. There you have a jurisdiction which appears to have no other function than that of adjusting the interests of the King and of his subjects, whereas, in reality, it thinks only of the former. For this reason, all the offices in any way appertaining to it are regarded as necessary, and it appears as if the financier had been overlooked in favour of the man who is useful to the King.

My kingdom pays as much, in proportion, as any other, and the taxes on it are very numerous, since my revenues are derived from Crown Lands, Woods, Mills, Subsidies, Tithes, Ferry-dues, Tolls, Salt, Fisheries, Game-licences, Stamped-paper, Stamp-Office and Registration of Deeds, Great and Little Seals, Forfeiture of Estate, Taxes on Employment, Excise—which includes the rights over every kind of commodity in general, coming into the towns, whether necessaries or luxuries, and over all merchandise—the duty of billeting soldiers, the money for recruits, and finally, the men and horses for the artillery.

In spite of this multiplication of taxes, which are exacted with the utmost rigour, my subjects do not complain, because everything is done in my name, and care is taken to give to my representatives a certain social position.

There are authors who have advanced the theory that it is a part of kingly policy to farm out all sources of revenue, because, by this means, the hatred of the people is diverted to the collectors (farmers) alone. But these authors have not considered that the hatred recoils little by little upon the protector of these agents.

For a true comprehension of finance, you should read the Memorial prepared by the Royal Council of my father, upon the demise of my grandfather.

The Memorial of the Council

The King enquires how, without overburdening his subjects, he can extinguish a debt of thirty millions?

Finance is the Monster of the fable. In every State contempt of it is a point of honour, yet in every State it is the object of the greatest courtship and flattery. This contradiction inflicts considerable wrong upon the governing Princes.

We must discover the truth in everything, and to this end let us examine this Monster.

What is Finance?

It is the collection of the revenues of a State, or else the expenditure of these same revenues.

In whose name are these revenues collected or expended?

In the King's name.

Whom does the King employ for the raising or expending the revenues?

His subjects.

What sort of subjects has the King to choose for this work?

Honest men.

Are honest men to be despised?

No.

Why then are financiers despised?

Because they are not honest.

Whose fault is this?

That is the great problem which certainly will embarrass your Ministers.

What results from all this?

That you have need of revenues and of men to raise them, and that it behoves Your Majesty to choose them well.

Two points of view in general regulate the conduct of men: honour and interest. On all the occasions when it is possible to pay them with honour, it is so much gain over interest. This is therefore a coinage of which a prince should make as much use as possible. But since in a well-regulated State the different currencies ought not to be confused, it is essential to give to this coinage the degrees of valuation proper to it. For the money of this metal bestowed upon a General must not be the same in form as that presented to the premier merchant of the realm.

In order to carry out this project, we have formulated the following plan:

We desire that there shall no longer be any forms of tax-farming in our kingdom:

(1) Because they are useless to us, and utterly opposed to our interests.

(2) Because they come with too much authority between us and our subjects.

(3) Because they prevent us from knowing the true condition of things with regard to our revenues and to our subjects themselves.

(4) Because the gains brought about by them increase luxury, and corrupt manners; excite the great to indignation, and vex the populace.

(5) Finally, because they are opposed to the project we have formed of imparting a certain lustre to everything connected, directly or indirectly, with our finances.

In order to prove to you the more completely the uselessness of these farmers-general, we will show you that three-fourths of them are not, and never could be, useful people, not only because they are without credit of themselves, but also because their funds are the property of the public. As to their abilities, the only skill allowed them by their state is that of stoutly maintaining their rights.

As for scruples, we have not yet been fortunate enough to find a company which has said to us: "We were mistaken when we made such and such an agreement with Your Majesty. We were reckoning for a gain of 20 per cent., and we have found that it amounted to 72 per cent."

If our farmers-general were only useless to us, it would yet be possible at a pinch to make use of their services, but, unfortunately, they are absolutely opposed to our interests, not only on account of the gains they make off us, but chiefly because they are the cause of our paying a huge interest. We will explain this to you in a few words.

We have calculated the amount of interest which we have paid to various companies for the past ten years, and we have found that the sum total amounts to sixty millions of livres. These companies were possessed of little or no capital, in consequence of which they have been obliged to borrow the funds for the advances which they have made to us at different times.

From whom have they borrowed?

From the public.

Why did the public lend to them?

Because they paid five to six per cent.

Why did they pay five to six per cent.?

Because the King gave ten per cent., and the same money brought them in a further fifteen per cent. of profit.

Why did the King give them ten per cent.?

Because they came between the King and his subjects, and by this means drew all the money to themselves.

Why did they draw all the money to themselves?

Because the public prefers to do business with individuals who are making big profits rather than with the King.

It is certain, therefore, that when there is no middleman, the King will be the recipient of the interest on the money?

Yes, without doubt, and we may conclude with certainty that the King has paid at least thirty millions too much on these sixty millions.

We have no need to strengthen our case with further arguments; you know its soundness, and you will admit that the Ministers of the King my father have been much more than foolish. In effect, they have not been content with abandoning large profits on the revenues of the King, but they have further paid interest as if they had not had the smallest resources. One might say that they permitted the financiers to treat their master much in the same way that money-lenders treat minors of good family, with this difference only, that the King has been obliged to enrich those from whom he wished to borrow, whereas the minors of good family have not altogether the same vigilance as the usurers.

Here is a scheme for execution in every part of our revenue, the administration of which has appeared to us injurious to our interests.

SUBSIDIES

This tax cannot be further extended, since in reality we take more than a third of the revenue. Neither could it be assessed with greater justice, since it has been settled according to the register of the general survey of lands; the only question, therefore, is as to its collection.

This impost was originally regarded as a voluntary contribution, one at the same time necessary for the maintenance of the State. It was money which was not destined for the coffers of the King, but only for those of the Government; for which reason the State

Frederick the Great

itself had sought the least costly methods of raising the tax.

Then came the creation of the offices of Receivers-General and of Local Receivers. These were given rights of commission on the funds, they were allowed to charge collection expenses, and in some measure they received absolute authority over this section.

To remedy the abuses which have followed the changes, we have enquired of every province what subsidies and tithes it contributed, including costs, and we have verified the amounts paid into our treasury. The province of Minden has sent us the subjoined Memorandum.

MEMORANDUM

The Province of MINDEN has paid to the KING:—

	livres.	livres.
In Subsidy	550,000	
Expenses	15,000	
		565,000

COSTS to the KING upon this:—

Paid to Receiver-General of the Province:
(1) In Appointments.............. 6,000
(2) In Commission at one-half per cent. 8,250[1]

To four Local Receivers of the Province:
(3) In Appointments at 1,500 livres each.................... 6,000
(4) In Commission at one-half per cent.................... 8,250[1]
(5) In Expenses on account of delayed payments.............. 15,000
                                                              ——— 43,500

NET REMAINDER for the KING................ 521,500

[1] The king's arithmetic in this memorandum is absolutely unintelligible.

Thus far the evil does not appear great, but this is what renders it considerable. The four Receivers have a year in which to pay the Receiver-General, and the Receiver-General has eighteen months in which to pay the King. During this time they are continuing to receive, and are putting out their money to interest. What is the result? We find ourselves always a year and a half behindhand; we are obliged to borrow at least a year's amount, in order to meet necessary expenses. To whom do we apply? To these very Receivers-General, who lend us our own money at ten per cent. Therefore,

	livres
From the sum of	521,500
we must take further, the sum of	55,000[1]
You will see that there will finally remain to us only the sum of	466,500

After very careful consideration, we have proposed to the Province of Minden that it should raise a mean amount of 20,000 livres, to be received by us direct at Berlin, in two equal payments, to be made, the first in the month of August, and the second in the month of February of the following year. This proposal the Province has accepted.

The following are the advantages which will accrue to the Province and to us.

The Province will gain:—

	livres.
Upon the Charges of 15,000 livres, at least	7,500
Upon the sum of 20,000 livres, a Grant for Expenses of Collection amounting to	5,000
TOTAL GAIN for the Province	12,500

[1] The king's arithmetic in this memorandum is absolutely unintelligible.

Frederick the Great

We shall gain:—	livres.
(1) On the Expenses of Collection and of Commissions..............................	8,500
(2) Being paid every six months, we shall, at the lowest calculation, have to borrow half the amount only. Thus on the 55,000 livres interest formerly paid to the Receivers, we will gain the half, which leaves to the King..................................	27,500
TOTAL GAIN for the King....................	36,000

EXCISE DUES

We have established the general levying of Excise, and we have found that it amounts to....		4,500,000
On which the Tax-farmers pay out:—	livres.	
(1) To the King..................	1,500,000	
(2) On advances of 1,500,000 five per cent......................	75,000	
(3) In Expenses of Administration...	2,225,000	
		3,800,000
Consequently, there remains a net profit to the Tax-farmers of............................		700,000

After having established the general system of collection, we have sent to each province the details of its payments in subsidies, and we have enquired of them what would be the most certain and the least costly method of collecting them. We cite you the reply of the Province of Magdeburg, because it appears to us to be the clearest and the most satisfactory.

THE REPLY OF THE PROVINCE OF MAGDEBURG

We have not been surprised by the enormous expenses entailed on the Province by the administration of the Excise Dues, but we should be much astonished

if the King did not accord us the liberty of paying him
the subsidies by subscription, and above all, after the
Report which we are about to lay before him.

		livres.
In the Province of Magdeburg the amount actually collected comes to....................		450,000
The Expenses of Administration are as follows:		
	livres.	
(1) For Four Directors at 6,000 livres...	24,000	
(2) For Four Travelling Inspectors at 2,400 livres.....................	9,600	
(3) For Twenty Town Receivers at 1,200 livres..........................	24,000	
(4) For 120 Travelling Agents at 800 livres............................	96,000	
(5) Compensations and Expenses of Official Reports....................	20,000	
(6) Expenses and Salaries of the Court of Excise.........................	30,000	
(7) Remittance of monies to the General Pay-Office........................	10,000	
		213,600
Consequently, there remains for the Tax-farmers..		236,400

of which 236,400 livres the King receives about 120,000
livres. Of what then is it a question? It is to give to
the King 120,000 livres of Excise Dues. But we do far
more than this; we give him 170,000 livres, and this is
how we do so.

We have made two taxes, one for the towns, and the
other for the country, and we have made a general calculation upon the different returns sent in by the
burgomasters of the towns and villages, and we have
found that every year the sales throughout the province have been as follows:—

	Flagons of Wine.	Flagons of Beer.	Flagons of Spirits.
In the Boroughs and Towns..	400,000	1,500,000	30,000
In the Villages and Hamlets..	100,000	800,000	12,000
	500,000	2,300,000	42,000

Totals:—

Beer.........................	2,300,000
Wine.........................	500,000
Spirits.......................	42,000
TOTAL AMOUNT................	2,842,000

According to the Two taxes which we impose:

FOR THE TOWNS:

	livres.	livres.
400,000 flagons of wine at 10 sous make...........................	200,000	
[1] 1,500,000 flagons of beer at 4 deniers make...........................	25,000	
30,000 flagons of spirits at 20 sous make...........................	30,000	
		255,000

FOR THE VILLAGES:

100,000 flagons of wine at 5 sous make..	25,000	
800,000 flagons of beer at 3 deniers make.	12,000	
12,000 flagons of spirits at 10 sous make.	6,000	
		43,000
		298,000

We have sent circular instructions to the Burgomasters of the towns, and others to those of the villages to the following effect:—

INSTRUCTIONS TO THE BURGOMASTERS OF MAGDEBURG[1]

GENTLEMEN,

By the returns which you have forwarded to us,

---

[1] The king's arithmetic is unintelligible.

it is an established fact that the dealers in wine, beer, and spirits sell each year in your town

133,000 pots of wine
800,000   "   " beer
15,000   "   " spirits.

We charge you, Gentlemen, to collect, in whatever way suits you best, the sum of 93,833 livres, 6 sous, 8 deniers, to wit:—

	livres.	s.	d.
For the 133,000 flagons of wine, at 10 sous...	66,500	–	–
For the 800,000 flagons of beer at 4 deniers[1].	13,333	6	8
For the 15,000 flagons of spirits, at 1 livre...	15,000	–	–
Equal to the Imposition..................	94,833	6	8

We give the Town, for Expenses of Collection, as making very nearly the consumption of a third of the

	livres.	s.	d.
Province............................	20,000	–	–
This will not yield to the coffers of the King more than....................	74,833	6	8
	94,833	6	8

And by this arrangement the King will not collect further taxes from your town. You will have the satisfaction of giving him 16,000 livres more than the Tax-farmers, and the privilege of adjusting the tax on yourselves as you desire, and you will gain about 43,000 livres a year.

[1] The king's arithmetic is unintelligible.

Frederick the Great

INSTRUCTIONS TO THE BURGOMASTERS OF VILLAGES[1]

SIR,

Following the Schedule which you have sent us, it is obvious that the average sale per annum in your Village amounts to—

400 flagons of wine
2000 " " beer
150 " " spirits.

We charge you, Sir, on your Village, by whatever method appears most suitable to the Villagers in Council for this purpose, to collect the sum of 425 livres.

	livres.
For 400 flagons of wine at 5 sous.................	100
For 2000 flagons of beer at 3 sous.................	250
For 150 flagons of spirits at 10 sous...............	75
	425

We give to the Village, for Expenses of Administration, 85 livres, in consequence of which it will only be reported to yield 340 livres. By this payment the King holds you exempt from further Customs dues, and you will have the advantage of giving him about 40 livres a year more than the Tax-farmers, and the privilege of taxing yourselves, and of gaining about 180 livres.

CONCERNING SALT[1]

The Tax-farmers give us yearly for Salt 900,000 livres. In virtue of this sum, we grant them the exclusive right of working the Salt-mines and of manu-

---

[1] The arithmetic is again unintelligible.

facturing Salt, throughout our Kingdom, of charging our subjects 5 sous a pound for Salt, and of forcing them to take so much Salt per annum. According to the returns and the consumption of Salt during the past year, the Tax-farmers have disposed of 18,000,000 pounds of Salt at 5 sous

		livres.
a pound, which amounts to....................		4,500,000
on which they have paid		
	livres.	
To the King.......................	900,000	
For working the Salt at 6 deniers the pound.........................	350,000	
Interest on advances at about 5 per cent...........................	350,000	
Expenses of Distribution and Salaries.	900,000	3,270,000
Consequently the Tax-farmers retain.........		1,230,000

METHOD OF WORKING

We have devised a simple method of working, which the cupidity of the Tax-farmers has rendered extremely simple. It is as follows:—

We have required in each Province a Statement of the amount of Salt which it was obliged to take into store, and having collated all the different Statements, we have drawn up a rule of division for the 900,000 livres which the King draws from this farming; that is to say, we have applied to the Province that portion of this sum which corresponded to the amount of Salt taken, taking everything into consideration, and then we have sent to each Province the following Memorandum:—

Frederick the Great

MEMORANDUM SENT TO THE PROVINCE OF MINDEN[1]

GENTLEMEN,

By the Report which you have sent, we see that your Province is obliged to purchase from the depots of the Farmers-General a million pounds of Salt per annum, and to pay them, at the rate of 5 sous the pound, 250,000 livres.

The King does not wish to use compulsion with his subjects in the matter of any commodity which is indispensably necessary to them, and from this moment he takes over the control of the Salt Mines, and will manufacture the Salt at his own expense, for sale to all alike and without distinction. He merely requires from you that you should send him yearly, direct and free of charges, the sum of 50,000 livres, making the 18th part of that of 900,000 livres given him by the Farmers-General, and which you yourselves pay since you take a million pounds of Salt, making also the eighteenth part of the consumption for one year.

But as by his project the King increases his revenue, and at the same time confers an advantage upon you, we propose to go into the matter with you in greater detail (more minutely).

	livres.
You take a million pounds of Salt every year, and you pay for it 5 sous per pound, which makes......	250,000
On this 250,000 livres the King receives only....	50,000
Consequently there remains for the farmers......	200,000
Through the enquiries which we have made, we know that the Tax-Farmers disburse on the	200,000

[1] The arithmetic is again unintelligible.

(1) For the production of a million livres.
pounds of Salt at 1 sou the pound..... 75,000
(2) Interest on advances both for the
75,000 livres and for the 50,000 livres
given to the King, about............. 6,800
(3) Expenses of Distribution at 1 sou
per pound........................ 50,000
—————
131,800

Leaving for the Tax-Farmers.................. 68,000

It is this 68,200 livres which the King proposes to divide with you and your Province, by giving the dealer for right of sale the 50,000 livres which it costs the Tax-Farmers in salaries for distribution of this commodity in your Province. We imagine that your dealers will be well satisfied.

Tobacco

sous.
We allow our tax-farmers to sell tobacco to the public at the rate per pound of........................... 45
It costs them the following:—

sous.
(1) Payment to Your Majesty.................. 10
(2) Purchase in leaf........................... 12
(3) Carriage.................................. 2
(4) Manufacture.............................. 3
(5) Packing (or making up) and waste........... 2
(6) Extraordinary expense and interest on advances.. 3
(7) Wages and expense of distribution............ 4
—— 36

There consequently remains as net gain to the tax-farmers on every pound........................... 9

According to the total of the past year, this consumption has amounted to eight million pounds. Thus, our Tax-farmers have made 3,600,000 livres.

In order to secure for ourselves a portion of these profits, we are establishing a General Depot in each Province, to which the Tobacco is brought in the first instance in leaf, to be then manufactured, and finally sold at a fixed price to whoever wants it.

According to the calculation we have ourselves made, based upon that of the Farmers-General, each

	sous.
pound should cost us not more than..........	20
(1) For the purchase in leaf.....................	12
(2) Carriage.................................	1
(3) Manufacture.............................	3
(4) Packing and waste........................	2
(5) Interest and advances.....................	2
	— 20
We shall sell it to the public at............	35
Consequently, we shall gain..............	15

which makes a gain of 2,000,000 livres for us.

There remains 10 sous, which will be re-absorbed in commerce, and which will be shared, naturally, between the public and the dealer, for the latter will certainly be content to make four or five sous per pound.

FORESTRY

	livres.
This Department is farmed for......	2,500,000
Upon this sum we pay.............	800,000

to an endless number of officials, created formerly for the purpose of keeping order, exclusive of the cost of their official reports, which are made at our expense, and which amount to more than 400,000 livres per annum.

	livres.
Therefore, from the sum of.........	2,500,000
we must deduct.................	1,200,000
Consequently there only remains to ourselves.....................	1,300,000

In order thoroughly to understand the value of this source of revenue, we have sent Surveyors into each Province, who have drawn plans of all our forests, have produced specimens of them, have analysed the qualities of the woods, have noted the price of each, and have observed the best method of selling them.

One can judge by the Report on one of our Provinces the result of their investigations throughout the Kingdom.

Province of Minden

Report Sent to the Council by the Surveyor

There are in this Province 8,000 acres of Wood. These 8,000 acres consist of three forests, to wit:—

	acres.
That of..	4,000
That of..	2,000
And that of.....................................	2,000

The forest of............is composed of

       2,000 acres of firs
       1,000 " " oaks
   and 1,000 " " beeches.

Its situation, close to the Weser, enables all the wood to be sold at a reasonable price, to wit:—

		livres.
That of Firs, which are cut down every sixty years, at........................	800	per acre.
That of Oaks, which may be cut down every twenty years, at..................	150	"
That of Beech, which one may cut down at the same periods, at..................	180	"

According to my calculations, cutting so regulated, will bring in:—

	livres.
Firs, about 33¾ acres at 800 livres, the sum of......	26,666
Oaks, about 50 acres, at 150 livres...............	7,500
Beech, about 50 acres, at 180 livres.............	9,000
TOTAL per annum............................	43,166

The Forest of..........is composed of 2,000 acres, to wit:—

	acres.
Oaks.........................	1,400
Beech........................	200
Chestnuts.....................	200
And White Wood...............	200

This Forest is not well situated, because there are no large rivers or big towns in the neighbourhood, thus I don't cut the wood for sale, but to make the following use of it:—

Every year I take 24 acres of Oaks, which I have made into planks,[1] and I find that after deducting all expenses each acre brings in 250 livres, making a total of 6,000 livres.

[1] Or stave-wood—*merrain* in the dictionary.

	livres.
Carried forward...............................	6,000
Then I take 13⅓ acres of beech and of white wood, because I have divided the 400 into thirty parts, and I make a lime-kiln, provided I find in the forest itself the right kind of material for this purpose. By the sale of the lime I find that each acre is worth, less expenses, 30 livres, which makes 13⅓ acres worth.................	400
Of the 200 acres of Chestnuts, I cut 8 acres every year, and I have them made into barrel hoops: I find that each acre brings in 80 livres, which makes on the 8 acres the sum of.........................	640
	7,040

The Forest of.......... is composed of

	acres.
Oaks.........................	600
Beeches......................	1,200
White Wood..................	200

It is situated in a plain, easy of access, and within easy reach of three small towns.

I divide the 600 acres of Oak into 100, and I find that I can cut 6 acres every year. Since these three small towns must of necessity supply themselves with wood and building material, I sell these six acres for..	livres 9,000
Carried forward.............................	7,040
" "	9,000
Of the 1,200 acres of Beech trees, I take 800, which I cut every 25 years, to make firewood, which makes 32 acres every year, which I sell at 160 livres, bringing in	5,120
For the 400 acres remaining of Beechwood, and the 200 acres of White Wood, I cut them every 13 years, making each year 15 acres, and I make them into brushwood, which is done up into large faggots, for the convenience of the poor. I find that the sale of this brings me in per acre 120 livres, making in all for the 150 acres...........................	6,000
TOTAL.....................	27,160

¹ The arithmetic is again unintelligible.

SCHEDULE OF THE DISTRICT OF .....

This District contains two large and enormous forests, which embrace a considerable extent of country. These two forests are situated partly on the plain, and partly on the mountain. They are both of them far distant from any large rivers, and have, properly speaking, no outlet, so that the property is useless to the King.

But the examination which has been made of these two forests has shown that they can be made use of.

(1) There are districts in which it would be an easy matter to establish glass and china works, because there is there plenty of fern and earth, and no lack of water.

(2) There are large streams, collected or dammed in good beds for the formation of canals, especially at the times when the snows are melting, or during the periods of the heavy rains.

In order that the undertaking may cost us nothing, a Company might be formed, wherein we would be represented by an Agent, and to which we would subscribe a quarter of the funds; this Company would make the necessary advances for the Canals, and for this purpose it would have the use of the wood for a period of...years.

As there are valleys which are situated at too great a distance from these canals, the woods there should be burnt out, and villages built on the clearings, which would soon be peopled, since the land will be excellent for pasture, and the inhabitants would find plenty of occupation in the regular felling of the wood which will be established, and in the upkeep of all the canals.

We believe this project to be good, Sire, because,

however weak may be the Navy of our Kingdom, it will be able to obtain thereby a great deal of wood, and even for export to France; which would be a matter of great importance to our dominions, since by this means we open up a very considerable source of exportation and of revenue.

MEMORANDUM OF THE POSTAL SERVICE TO THE KING

We have no suggestions to make concerning the Administration of the Postal Service, because, all things considered, it is good in our Kingdom. The only transaction which we would beg of you is to place this department under the Excise, since you would then gain yearly at least the amount of the tax-farmer's profit. You are the better able to do this, that the department is a well-equipped machine and not liable to much change. Moreover, the same employés would serve under the Excise, and the general management can be left to the present official.

Your Postal Service is in the hands of six tax-farmers and a dozen subordinates (partners).

	livres.	
The tax-farmers each make at least 60,000 livres, which for the six amounts to		360,000
The 12 subordinates each make 15,000 livres or together		180,000
In all		540,000
From this amount we must take that of		140,000
to wit:—	livres.	
For the General Manager	60,000	
Four Directors-General attached to the Excise Office	80,000	
There remains as profit to Your Majesty	140,000	400,000

Frederick the Great

POST-HOUSES

The Postal Service is divided into two branches: Letter-Posts and Post-Houses.

The Post-Houses are onerous to us, and the Letter-Posts are not so advantageous as they should be. We have, therefore, to find a means of improving conditions in every respect.

The Post-Houses are a burden to us, because they involve for all the Post-masters salaries exception from Poll-tax, and qualification for compensation in case of accident, and because no profit accrues to us therefrom.

Let us now examine the reasons which led my father to institute this arrangement.

Vanity was the principal reason. He believed that it appertained to the dignity of a king to have public posts established in all parts of his kingdom. He did not regard these establishments as existing only for the distribution of letters, but much more for giving greater facilities to the nobility and to wealthy commoners for the display of pomp.

The following are the arrangements which we have made in this matter:—

(1) We have taken an exact survey of all the roads in the Kingdom; and after a complete and very minute enquiry, having found four hundred posting-routes which are hardly ever used by carriages or coaches, we have reduced them to one stage-horse and three saddle-horses each.

(2) As our intention is to revive a branch of industry in our Kingdom, we desire, so to speak, to force everyone to use the public conveyances, and to this end we are reducing the remainder of the posts to half the

number of horses, and at the same time doubling the cost of posting to everyone except our ordinary and extraordinary couriers, our Ambassadors, our Generals, and our Agents, on Royal business requiring expedition.

By these two regulations, the Post-masters will no longer be surcharged, and the couriers, being paid double by the public will certainly profit, to an extent which should enable us to take from them exemption from Poll-tax, and to reduce their salaries by one-half.

That is the scheme, and this is the manner in which it should be of use to us and to the public.

To us, because it is certain that upon two thousand Post-masters, we should gain

	livres.
through diminution of salaries, about.............	100,000
and through rescinding their tax-exemption.........	300,000
making a total of.................................	400,000

With regard to the Public: We presume that there are yearly 4,000 persons to whom posting is rather a matter of appearances than of necessity; these 4,000 persons will save, one way and another, at least 72 livres each, which makes in all the sum of..

	livres.
	288,000
These same 4,000 persons by travelling in the public conveyances will benefit the drivers and the innkeepers to the extent of at least 30 livres each, making in all................................	120,000
Making a total of.................................	408,000

We would observe to Your Majesty that the public service will in no way suffer, since upon all the frequented routes we shall leave the posting well enough equipped for no loss of time to be occasioned.

STAMP OFFICE AND REGISTRATION OF DEEDS[1]

After a labour of some length, and the compilation of an abstract of all the registers of the past year, we have arrived at some measure of information as to the amount brought into the revenue by each Controller, and we have found that, all told, these tax-farmers raise an amount of.. **livres.** 4,000,000

of which four millions they spend: **livres.**
- Given to us..................... 2,200,000
- In Salaries..................... 400,000
- Extraordinary Expenses........... 200,000
- Advances at the rate of 5 per cent... 80,000

                                    3,280,000

Profits....................................... 720,000

We shall oblige each individual Receiver to bring us the same sum that he brought to the Farmers–General, paying it direct and free of cost of sending, and we will give him a third more salary; which might make a sum of.............. **livres.** 150,000

We shall nominate further four Directors-General at a salary of 25,000 livres each, in all.............. 100,000

And 12 Inspectors-General at 6,000 livres each...... 72,000

Leaving for the King......................... 322,000

                                    livres.

By this operation, we gain, in the first place...... 720,000
Of which, in order to ensure a thorough service, we spend out................................ 322,000

Leaving a balance for us of..................... 398,000

STAMPED PAPER

Throughout our dominions during the past year there have been sold 16,000,000 sheets of stamped paper, yielding, at 1 sou the sheet, the sum of..................... **livres. s. d.** 800,000

[1] Frederick's addition is hopeless.

		livres	s.	d.
The Tax-farmers have paid us......... ..		200,000		
The 16,000,000 sheets of paper have cost them, at 4 deniers the sheet...	livres. s. d. 133,333 6 8			
For Stamp, at 1 denier per sheet.............	33,333 6 8			
Distribution at 2 denier per sheet.............	66,666 13 4			
Advances of about 400,000 livres at 5 per cent.....	20,000			
Office and Extraordinary Expenses.............	50,000	303,333	6	8
Remains to the Farmers-General..........		503,333	6	8

MODUS OPERANDI (Schedule)

	livres	s.	d.
Every year there are manufactured in one of our mills 16,000,000 sheets of paper at 3 deniers the sheet, amounting to the sum of................................	100,000	0	0
These are stamped at 1 denier per sheet.....	33,333	6	8
(3) In every Province we establish a General Depôt in the office of the Registrar-General of the chief town, who is responsible for the distribution. We allow him to charge 1 denier per sheet; those who distribute after him being allowed to charge 2 deniers per sheet, the total cost amounts to 3 deniers per sheet, in all..................	100,000	0	0
Making a full total of.....................	233,333	6	8

By this you will see that by selling our paper ourselves, we shall make, at 2 sous a sheet, 566,666 livres 13 sous 4 deniers.

But, as our principal object is for the Public to gain as well as ourselves, it shall not be sold at more than 1 sou the sheet, and thus the Public will profit by the **transaction to the amount of 141,660 livres, and we** ourselves to the amount of 425,000 livres, instead of the 200,000[1] livres which the tax-farmer gives us.

CUSTOMS-DUTY ON FOREIGN GOODS

	livres.
The Tax-farmers in this department raise every year the sum of..............................	1,200,000
They hand over to us.......................	400,000
So that there remains to them................	800,000

The object of these Customs was to impede foreign trade, so that the money should not leave the Kingdom, and to oblige the inhabitants to dress in material manufactured in the Kingdom. By degrees luxury has increased, and money has become more plentiful, so that it has become really expedient to manufacture these same goods in the country.

We have manufactures of every description. The owners of these factories have the deepest interest in impeding the sale of foreign goods. Why, then, should we not come to an understanding with them as to the matter of Customs Dues? The following is the action which we have taken in the matter.

We have had an exact Abstract of the different goods which come into the Kingdom each year made, as well as of the duties which are collected upon these goods.

From this enquiry it appears that our Tax-farmers receive at least

	livres.
On Silk materials, Ribbons and the like........	400,000
On Cloth and other woollen goods.............	400,000
On Cloth of Gold and of Silver, and on Gold and Silver jewellery..........................	200,000
On Iron and Steel goods	100,000
And on Copper and Tin goods.................	100,000
Making a total of..........................	1,200,000

[1] The arithmetic is again faulty.

Having made this Abstract, we have proposed to all the Manufacturers to pay us, direct and free of all Charges, the sum of 600,000 livres; and we have promised them, in the name of His Majesty, a Law, forbidding, under the most rigorous penalties, anyone soever, whether of His Majesty's subjects or a foreigner, bringing into our realm any goods for which there are factories established in our dominions; and we have given them permission to carry this law into effect themselves and through their accredited agents. And in order to prevent any confusion in the matter of the payment of the 600,000 livres, we have put a tax upon every species of manufactured goods: to wit:—

	livres.
All Silken Manufactures, Materials, Ribbons, and the like	2,000,000
All Manufactures of Cloth and Other Woollen Goods	200,000
Gold and Silver Goods and Jewellery	50,000
Copper and Tin Goods	50,000
In all	2,300,000

All the manufacturers have agreed to this proposition, and therefore we gain 200,000 livres, but it is impossible to estimate the benefits which we shall confer by this arrangement, in the first place, because money will no longer be taken out of the country, and secondly, because our subjects will profit to the same extent by each other as the foreigners formerly did by them.

OCTROI DUTIES IN THE TOWNS

We leave unaltered the established Octroi duties in the Towns, upon commodities and goods of which we have made no mention. They are just and necessary, because it is through them that trade contributes to the upkeep of the State. But we propose that each town should compound these dues. We know, more or less, by the Abstract of the Registers of these districts how much they can afford to pay, so that we should not be liable to any injury by this arrangement.

My father, after having examined the Scheme for this new Administration, followed his own opinion on the subject, and continued to collect the Subsidies upon the basis of the Land-Survey register, and allowed the local and general receivers to continue.

To simplify the administration of all these taxes, payment of toll was permitted at the town gates on tobacco, coffee, tea, chocolate, sugar, wheat, flour, spirits, beer, liqueurs, and generally, on all the necessities and luxuries of life.

For this purpose he established in every town an Excise Office, the staff of which, in large towns, consisted of a Receiver, a Cashier, a Superintendent, an Inspector, and ten clerks, and in small towns, of a Receiver and two clerks. He then formed Departments, over which he placed Commissaries.

To ensure respect for his employees, he gave them honourable social rank, which made it possible for him to insist on their taking lower salaries, and being content with modest profits.

With regard to Salt, he undertook the manufacture of it himself, distributing it at his own cost and expense.

The Stamping of Documents was a Department which he considered too delicate for his interference. He would not even touch that of Stamped Paper.

As regards the Forestry scheme, he adopted it more or less as it stood.

This new source of revenue only brought him in a profit of two millions.

And it was only by putting the interior of his house in order that he placed himself in a position to pay his debts. It is true that he introduced into it an order so economical that it could not be improved upon.

So long as I have had any money I have never thought about my finances. It is only since this War that this subject has claimed my constant attention.

I should like to continue further with you the Memorial of the Council of my father, but circumstances do not permit of my doing so, and I have not time to enter into such long and minute particulars; in the meantime, this is what I myself have done:

I have suggested to all the Commissaries of the Department to compound with all the towns. I have instituted a reform amongst all the Tax-collectors, and I have lowered their commission by one-half per cent.; all this will bring me in about 20,000,000 livres.

Secondly, I have found means to establish the poll-tax in those provinces which were the least overburdened, on the pretext of equalizing the impositions for payment of contributions. This little ruse will bring me in about 400,000 livres a year.

ARMY

	livres.
By retrenching five men per company, I make a yearly gain of......	1,000,000
On the 2 sous which I deduct from each soldier for commissariat bread, I save.........................	600,000
On hair powder and lodging.....	720,000
On Clothing..................	800,000
On Riding Hacks..............	180,000
On Staffs, Governments and Commands........................	300,000
In all......................	3,600,000

When I was certain of economizing 6,000,000 a year, I began to think of paying off my debts, and this is how I do so:

	livres.
Reckoning everything, I am in debt for........................	100,000,000;

the point is how to settle for this amount.

To this end, I borrow from the Dutch, in four years, at 4 per cent., the sum of......................	74,057,500

I add to this sum that of my savings.......................... 24,000,000 livres. and with the two I repay the 100,000,000 livres[1] of my debt.

When this transaction is concluded, I shall take out another loan of 60,843,025 livres, at 3 per cent.; I shall add to this amount 12,000,000 livres of savings; and I hope that in two years I shall find myself in a position to repay the 74,057,500 livres.[1] In this way, by the year 1771, I shall only owe, by the reduction of the interests, the sum of 60,843,025 livres. The subjoined table will afford you proof of this.

If there is no War in 1771, what will become of all these Repayments? That is the moment, my dear nephew, for which I am most earnestly looking, in order to introduce into my realm a new kind of currency.

I intend to circulate among the public a certain amount of paper; if this is taken up, I shall increase the amount; and if it is not taken up, I shall withdraw it, rather than allow it to become depreciated. I shall try this experiment several times, and I am firmly convinced that in the end money (specie) will become (a glut?) and the paper will take its place (or will rise?).

This transaction is a very delicate one, for, strictly speaking, paper has only a momentary and uncertain vogue. But it is very useful when one knows how to make good use of it.

[1] The king's arithmetic is again unintelligible.

TABLE[1]

SHOWING REPAYMENT OF 100,000,000 LIVRES DEBT BY THE REDUCTION OF INTEREST, AND THE ECONOMIES EMPLOYED IN THIS REPAYMENT

Date of loan.	Amounts due. livres.	Interest at 5 per cent. livres.	Amount borrowed from Dutch and Prussians. livres.	Economies effected for repayments. livres.	Interest on the loans at 4 per cent. livres.	Amounts repaid. livres.	Advantage gained by repayment livres.	Observations as to fate of money repaid livres.
1765	100,000,000	5,000,000	20,000,000	6,000,000	800,000	26,500,000	500,000	This money is put into general circulation.
1766	73,500,000	3,675,000	20,000,000	6,000,000	800,000	26,500,000	500,000	
1767	47,000,000	2,350,000	20,000,000	6,000,000	800,000	26,500,000	500,000	
1768	20,500,000	1,025,000	14,057,500	6,000,000	562,300	20,500,000	442,500	
	241,000,000	12,050,000	74,057,500	24,000,000	2,962,300	100,000,000	1,942,500	
SECOND LOAN.								
1769	74,057,500	at 4 per cent. 2,962,300	10,000,000	20,000,000	at 3 per cent. 6,000,000	900,000	36,600,000	60,000
1770	37,457,500	1,498,300	10,843,025	20,000,000	6,000,000	925,292	37,457,500	608,430
			20,843,025					

[1] I have not attempted to check these figures.—D. S.

If I can once succeed in launching it properly, I shall attempt the plan of repaying the loans partly in coin and partly in paper; and then, in three years I shall be able to extinguish the 60,843,025 livres.

The Life of Frederick the Great
By
Heinrich von Treitschke

The Life of Frederick the Great
By
Heinrich von Treitschke

FREDERICK WILLIAM'S reign fell in the miserable, Bœotian, idea-less age of the Peace of Utrecht; the small tricks of Fleury, Alberoni, and Walpole governed European politics. The upright Prince was helpless amid the cunning intrigues of the diplomatists. With old-German fidelity he held to his Kaiser, wanted to lay swords and pistols in the cradles of his children, in order to banish foreign nations from the Imperial soil. How often, with the beer-jug of the Fatherland in his hand, had he cried out his ringing: "Vivat Germania, Teutscher Nation!" Unsuspecting by nature, he now had to experience how the Court of Vienna, with its two ambitious neighbours, Hanover and Saxony, would come to a secret understanding on the division of Prussia, and how they would then help the Albertiners to the crown of Poland, deliver Lorraine to the French, and in his own home stir up discord between father and son, while they at last treacherously tried to wrest from him his right of succession to Berg and Ostfriesland.

So for his whole life he was pushed backwards and forwards between enemies and false friends; only at the end of his days did he see through Austria's cunning, and admonish his son to avenge a betrayed father. But at foreign courts it was said that the King stood continually on the watch with his gun at full cock, without ever letting it go off; and when occasionally a latent fear of the sentry at Potsdam overcame the other Germans, they were cheered by the sneer: "The Prussians won't shoot as quickly as all that!"

But the sneering was silenced when Prussia found a ruler who, by the happy practical sense of the Hohenzollerns, with a sense of the possible united the daring and clear vision of genius.

The bright sunshine of youth illuminates the beginning of the Frederician period, when at last, after much faltering and trepidation, the obstinate mass of the benumbed German world got on the move again, and the mighty contrasts which it hid measured themselves in the necessary struggle.

Since the days of that Lion of the Midnight Sun Germany had had no picture of a hero to whom the entire nation could look up with awe; but he who now, in proud freedom, as once Gustavus Adolphus had done, strode through the middle of the Great Powers, and forced the Germans to believe again in the wonder of heroism, he was a German.

The mainspring in this mighty nature is the ruthless, terrible German directness. Frederick gives himself as he is, and sees things as they are. As in the long row of volumes of his letters and writings there is not one line in which he attempts to extenuate his deeds, or to adorn his own picture for posterity, so his statesmanship, even if it did not despise the small arts and ruses of the age as means to an end, bears the stamp of his royal frankness.

As often as he draws his sword, he announces with candid exactitude what he demands from the enemy, and lays down his weapon only when he has reached his goal. From the moment that he awakes to thinking, he feels himself glad and proud that he is the son of a free century, which, with the torch of reason, shines in upon the dusty corners of a world of old prejudices and lifeless traditions; he has the picture of the Sun-god, who climbs up through the morning clouds, victorious, on the ceiling of his gay Rheinsberger Hall.

With the bold confidence of an apostle of enlightenment, he approaches the apparitions of historical life, and tests each one, to see how it will stand the judgment of a penetrating intellect. In the severe struggles of the various States for power, he notices only realities, and esteems only force cleverly used with presence of mind. "Negotiations without weapons are like music without instruments," he says calmly, and on the news of the death of the last Habsburg, he asks his advisers, "I give you a problem to solve; when one has the advantage, shall one make use of it or not?"

The swaggering impotence which poses as power, the senseless privileges which make a show of historical right, the fainéants, who mask their helplessness behind empty platitudes, could never find a more arrogant contemner; and nowhere could this inexorable realism operate so cleansingly and disturbingly, so revolutionarily, as in the great fable of the (Holy) Roman Empire. Nothing could be more pitiless than Frederick's derision of the holy Majesty of the Kaiser Francis, who is toddled round on the apron-strings of his wife, and (a worthy King of Jerusalem) executes lucrative contracts for the armies of the Queen of Hungary: nothing more fierce than his mocking of "the phantom" of the Imperial army, of the conceited futility of the minor Courts, of the peddling formalism of "these cursed old fogies of Hanover," of the empty pride of the estate-less petty feudal nobility (*Junkertum*) in Saxony and Mecklenburg, of "the whole breed of princes and peoples in Austria"—"who bends his knee to the great ones of this world, he knows them not!"

In full consciousness of superiority, he holds out the healthy reality of his modern State beside the shadowy conceptions of the Imperial Law; a sullen ill-nature speaks from his letters when he lets "the pedants of Regensburg" experience the iron necessity of war. Frederick fulfils in the deed what the wrangling publicists of the past centuries, Hippolithus and Severinus, have attempted only with words; he holds the "fearfully corpse-like face of Germany" up to the mirror, proves before all the world the irretrievable rottenness of the Holy (Roman) Empire.

Well-meaning contemporaries may have blamed him, because he delivers up the time-honoured community to ridicule; posterity thanks him, for he brings truth to honour again in German politics, as Martin Luther once brought it in German thought and faith.

Frederick had appropriated that severe Protestant view of German history and Imperial politics which had prevailed among the freer intellects of Prussia since Pufendorf and Thomasius, and then, with the embittering experiences of his tyrannized youth, cultivated them further, rigorously and independently.

In the rising of the Schmalkaldener, in the Thirty-Years' War, in all the confusion of the last two centuries, he saw nothing but the unceasing struggle of German freedom against the despotism of the House of Austria, which governed the weaker princes as slaves "with an iron rod," and left only the strong free to do as they chose. Not without arbitrariness he arranged the facts of history according to this one-sided view; one-sidedness turned towards light and life is, after all, the privilege of the creative genius. To bring the old struggle to a victorious end seemed to him the problem of the Prussian State. In his younger years he remained still true to Protestant things: he prized the glorious duty of the house of Brandenburg "to promote the Protestant religion everywhere in Germany and in Europe," and remarked, full of displeasure, in Heidelberg, how here in the old dominions of our Church the monks and priests of Rome again carried on their existence.

Even afterwards, when he estranged himself from the Church, and disdainfully condemned the mediocre parsons' outlooks of Luther and Calvin, from the height of his self-sure philosophical outlook, the conviction remained alive in him that his State, with every root of its being, belonged to the Protestant world. He knew how all the accomplices of the Vatican worked secretly for the annihilation of the new great Protestant Power; he knew that his human ideal of religious toleration, the right of the individual to attain salvation in his own fashion, was possible in the first place only on a footing of Protestantism; he knew that in new and worldly forms he was carrying on the struggles of the sixteenth century, and above his last work, the outline or sketch for the German Princes' League (*Fürstenbund*), he wrote the expressive inscription: "After the pattern of the rules for the League of Schmalkalden."

The earliest of the political writings of Frederick preserved for us show us the eyes of the eighteen-year-old boy already turned to that sphere of political life in which he was to unfold his highest and most characteristic powers—the question of higher politics. The Crown-Prince examined the position of his State in the world, found the situation of his divided provinces heavily imperilled, and, still half-joking and in high spirits, drew up bold calculations as to how the remote provinces were to be rounded off, that they should no longer find themselves "so lonely, without company."

Only a short time, and the unripe youthful projects returned as deep and mighty purposes; three years before his ascension to the throne he already saw, with the clairvoyance of genius, the great path of his life lying open before him:

It seems [so he writes] that Heaven has appointed the King to make all preparations which wise precautions before the beginning of a war demand. Who knows, if Providence has not reserved it for me to make a glorious use of these war-means at some future time, and to convert them to the realization of the plans for which the foresight of my father intended them?

He noticed that his State tottered in an untenable position midway between the small States and the Great Powers, and showed himself determined to give a definite character to this anomalous condition (*décider cet être*): it had become a necessity to enlarge the territory of the State, and *corriger la figure de la Prusse*, if Prussia wished to stand on her own feet and bear the great name of Kingdom with honour.

From generation to generation his ancestors had given the House of Austria faithful military service, always conscientiously disdaining to profit by the embarrassments of her neighbour; ingratitude, betrayal, and contempt had been their reward. Frederick himself had experienced heavily in his oppressed youth "the arrogance, the presumption, the disdainful pride of this bombastic Court of Vienna"; his heart was sworn to hatred against "the Imperial gang," who with their crawling and lying had estranged his father's heart from him.

His untamable pride sprang up when, at the paternal court, there was no cold refusal forthcoming to the presumptions of Austria: he wrote angrily that the King of Prussia should be like the noble palm-tree, of which the poet said: "If you wish to fell it, it lifts its proud crest." At the same time he followed with a watchful eye the dislocation of power in the political system, and had arrived at the conclusion that the old policy of the balance of power of the States of Europe had wholly outlived itself; since the victories of the War of the Spanish Succession it was no longer the opportune time to battle with Austria and England against the Bourbons.

The policy now was to lift the new German State "through the frightfulness of its weapons" to such a degree of power that it might maintain its independence against every great neighbour, even against the Imperial House.

So the much misused expression "German freedom" received a new, nobler meaning in Frederick's mouth. It no longer meant that dishonourable minor-princes' policy, which called on foreign countries for help against the Kaiser and betrayed the boundaries of the Empire to the alien; it meant the uplifting of a great German Power, which would defend the Fatherland in east and west, but of its own free will, independent of the authority of the Empire.

For centuries it had been the rule that he who was not good Austrian must be good Swede, like *Hippolithus a Lapide*, or good French, like the princes of the Rhine-League, or good English, like the kindred of the House of Guelph; even the Great Elector, in the frightful pressure between superior neighbours, could only maintain an independent position from time to time. It was Frederick's work that beside both those equally ruinous tendencies, the veiled and the unveiled foreign lordship, a third tendency should arise, a policy which was only Prussian, and nothing further; *to it* Germany's future belonged.

It was not the method of this hater of empty words to talk much of the Fatherland; and yet there lived in his soul a sensitive, gruffly-rejecting national pride, grown inseparably with his authoritative self-reliance and his pride of birth. That foreign nations should play the master on German soil was to him like an offence to his personal honour and the illustrious blood in his veins, which the philosophical King, naïve as genius is, still prized highly.

When the astonishing confusion of German affairs occasionally drove him to an alliance with foreigners, he never promised the foreign Powers a sod of German land, never let them misuse his State for their purposes. His whole life long he was accused of faithless cunning because no treaty or league could make him resign the right of deciding for himself.

All the Courts of Europe spoke with resentment of the *travailler pour le roi de Prusse;* being used of old to govern the life of Germany, they could scarcely grasp that at last the resolute selfishness of an independent German State was again opposed to their will. The royal pupil of Voltaire had begun for the German State the same work of emancipation as Voltaire's rival, Lessing, accomplished for our poetry.

Already in his youthful writings he condemns in sharp words the weakness of the Holy (Roman) Empire, which had opened its Thermopylæ, Alsace, to the foreigner; he is angry with the Court of Vienna, which has delivered up Lorraine to France; he will never forgive the Queen of Hungary for letting loose the wild pack of hounds, those ornaments of the East, the Jazygiens, Croatians, and the Tolpatschians, on the German Empire, and for the first time calling up the Muscovite barbarians to interfere in Germany's domestic affairs.

Then during the seven years his German pride and hate relieves itself in words of furious scorn. To the Russians, who plunder the peasants of his new *mark* (province), he sends the blessing: "Oh, could they only submerge themselves with one spring in the Black Sea, headlong, the hindmost last, they themselves and their memory!" And when the French overflow the Rhineland, he sings (in the French language, it is true) that ode which reminds one of the ring of the War of Liberation:

> Bis in seine tiefste Quelle,
> Schäumt der alte Rhein vor Groll,
> Flucht der Schmach, dass seine Welle
> Fremdes Joch ertragen soll!
>
> (Down to his deepest spring,
>   The old Rhine foams with rage,
>   Curses the outrage, that his waves
>   A foreign yoke must bear.)

"Prudence is very inclined to preserve what one possesses, but courage alone knows how to acquire"—with this voluntary confession Frederick betrayed in his Rheinsberger days how his innermost being forced him to quick resolution, to stormy audacity. To do nothing by halves seemed to him the first duty of the statesman, and of all imaginable resolutions, the worst to him was—to take none. But he showed his German blood in that he knew how to restrain his fiery impetuous activity at the outset with cold, calm calculation. He who felt the heroic power of an Alexander in him, assigned himself to achieve something lasting in the narrow circle in which Fate had placed him.

In war he now and then gave rein to his fiery spirit, demanded the impossible from his troops, and failed through arrogant contempt of the enemy: as a statesman he preserved always a perfect moderation, a wise self-restraint, which rejected every adventurous plan at the threshold.

Never for a moment was he duped by the thought of breaking loose his State from the decayed German community; the position of being a State of the Empire did not cramp him in the freedom of his European policy; it preserved for him the right to have a finger in the destiny of the Empire; therefore he wished to keep his foot in the stirrup of the German steed. Still less did it occur to him to reach out for the Emperor's crown himself.

After the prophecies of the court astrologers of the Great Elector, there always remained alive in the neighbourhood of the Hohenzollerns the vague, dim, obscure presentiment that this House was destined at some time to bear the sceptre and sword of the Holy (Roman) Empire; the firebrands, Leopold von Dessau and Winterfeldt, presumed occasionally to hail their royal hero as the German Augustus. But he knew that his secular State could not support the Roman crown, that it could only involve the parvenu among the Powers in disputes which there was no prospect of solving, and remarked drily: "For us it would only be a fetter."

Scarcely had he ascended to the throne, when

German affairs entered on that great change which Pufendorf's prophetic vision had already denoted as the only possible ground for a thorough reform of the Empire. The old Kaiser-House died out, and before the flaming vision of the young King, who held the only systematic war-power of Germany in his hands, there opened a world of alluring visions, which would have inspired a less profound, less collected nature to extravagant dreams. Frederick felt vividly the deep solemnity of the hour: "Day and night," he confessed, "the fate of the Empire lies on my heart. I alone can and must hold it upright."

He was determined that this great moment must not fly without giving the Prussian State full freedom of movement, a place in the council of the Great Powers; but he divined also how incalculably, owing to the covetousness of the foreign neighbours, and the helpless dissensions in the Empire, the position of Germany must be affected as soon as the monarchy of the Habsburgs fell to pieces. Therefore he wished to spare Austria, and contented himself with bringing forward the most important of the carefully pondered pretensions of his House. Alone, without vouchsafing one word to the foreign Powers on the watch, with an overwhelming invading force, he broke into Silesia.

Germany, used to the solemn reflections and cross-reflections of her Imperial lawyers, received with astonishment and indignation the doctrine that the rights of States were only to be maintained by active power. Then the conqueror offered to procure the Imperial Crown for the husband of Maria Theresa, and to fight for the integrity of Austria against France. Only the opposition of the Court of Vienna drives him farther to comprehensive plans for the reform of the Empire which remind one of Waldeck's daring dreams.

It was not Frederick who created German duality, with which the contemporary- and after-world reproached him; the dualism had lasted since Charles V, and Frederick was the first who earnestly tried to abolish it.

As soon as the understanding with the Court of Vienna proved impossible, the King was seized with the daring thought of wresting the Imperial Crown for ever from the House of Austria, breaking the last chain which linked this dynasty to Germany. He approached the Bavarian Wittelsbachs, the only House among the more powerful German princely families who, like the Hohenzollerns, governed German land alone, and like them, saw in Austria their natural enemy

He first founded that alliance between the two great pure German States which has since then so often, and always for the welfare of the Fatherland, been renewed. The Elector of Bavaria received the Imperial dignity, and Frederick hoped to ensure a firm support for the new Empire, which he himself called "my work," in the crown of Bohemia.

And soon in Berlin, as in Munich, awakened again that saving thought of secularization which inevitably forced itself up as soon as a healing hand was laid on the languishing body of the Empire. The work of strengthening the power of the greater secular States of the Empire, which Frederick recognized as its only vital members, at the cost of the theocratic and republican territories, was in progress.

There was an attempt to realize a purely secular statecraft in the political ideas of the Reformation. Certain ecclesiastical districts of Upper Germany (South Germany) were to be secularized, and various Imperial cities were to be attached to the dominions of the neighbouring princes.

With good reason Austria complained how seriously this Bavarian Empire, guided by Prussia, threatened to harm the Nobility and the Church. If these crude thoughts entered into life, the German dualism was as good as done with; the constitution of the Empire, even if the forms remained, was transformed.

Germany became an alliance of temporal princes under Prussia's governing influence. The ecclesiastical States, the Imperial cities, the swarm of small counts and princes, robbed of the support of the Habsburgs, fell into decay, and the hostile element in the heart of the Empire, the Crown of Bohemia, was conquered for the Germanic civilization. So Germany could by her own strength accomplish that necessary revolution which the decree of foreign countries, two generations later, insultingly imposed on her. But the House of Wittelsbach, estranged all the same from German life by its hereditary connection with France as by the severity of the Catholic unity of faith, showed in time a lamentable incapability. The nation failed to understand the promise of the moment. On a *Rundreise* round the Empire the King gained such a disconcerting insight into the dissensions, the avarice, the slavish fear of the small Courts, that he learned to moderate his German hopes for ever; even his own power could not suffice to wholly break the gallant opposition of the Queen of Hungary.

The second Silesian war ended, in spite of the triumphs of Hohenfriedberg and Kesselsdorf, in the restoration of the Austrian Empire. It remained in its constitution-less confusion, Francis of Lorraine ascended to the Imperial throne on the death of Charles VII, and the old alliance between Austria and the Catholic majority on the Imperial Diet was renewed.

The solution of German dualism miscarried; more hostile than ever, the parties in the Empire separated. However, the King remained sure of a lasting advantage: the position of Prussia as a Great Power. He had saved the Bavarians from downfall, had strengthened the forces of his country by more than a third, had broken with a bold stroke the long chain of Habsburg-Wettin provinces which surrounded the Prussian State in the south and east, and humiliated the proud Kaiser-House for the first time before a prince of Germany. For all his victories he had to thank his own strength alone, and he met the old Powers with such determined pride that Horatio Walpole himself had to admit that this Prussian King had now the scales of the balance of power in Europe in his hands.

Saxony, Bavaria, Hanover, all the Central-States, who had till this been contending with the Crown of Prussia, had been for ever thrown into the second line through the Silesian wars, and high above the countless small rivalries which cleft the Empire, rose the one question: Prussia or Austria?

The question of Germany's future had taken definite form. The King now looked down on the tumult of the German (Imperial) States from a clear elevation. He liked giving to offensive demands the mocking answer, did one take him perhaps for a Duke of Gotha or for a Rhine Prince? He played already to the small neighbours the rôle of the well-meaning patron and protector, which he had defined as the noble duty of the strong in his Anti-Machiavellism, and already a small Prussian Party gathered in the Reichstag, and the North-German Courts let their princes serve in the army of the King.

In the meantime, the new acquisition grew, together with the Monarchy, surprisingly quickly; the State experienced for the first time on a wide sphere those advantages and improvements which it has since then preserved everywhere in German and half-German countries. The fresh powers of the modern world made their entry even into the most neglected province, held down with temporal and ecclesiastical oppression; the dominion of the aristocracy was supplanted by monarchical bureaucracy, nepotism by strict justice, intolerance by religious liberty, the deep soul-slumber of priestly teaching by German educational systems; the dull servile peasant learned to hope for a morning again and his King forbade him to kiss the robe of the official, kneeling.

No other State in that century of struggles for supremacy presented such many-sided, such dignified problems. Only the peaceful work effected by the government gave the conquest of Silesia moral justification, and demonstrated that that much-blamed hazardous enterprise had been a German achievement. The glorious border-country, already half flooded with foreign influences, was given back to the German nation through the Prussian régime.

Silesia was the only one of the German-Austrian hereditary countries where the policy of a single faith could not boast of a full conquest. With invincible tenacity, the light-hearted, gay German race in the valleys of the Riesen Mountains resisted the bloody deeds of the Lichtenstein dragoons as they resisted the persuasive powers of the Jesuits. The majority of the Germans remained true to the

Frederick the Great 147

Protestant faith; oppressed and neglected, robbed of all its possessions, the Evangelical Church prolonged a miserable life; only the threats of the Crown of Sweden provided them with the few churches which remained to them, in addition to the possession of various *Gnadenkirchen*.[1]

The Catholic Poles of Upper Silesia and the Czech colonists, whom the Imperial Court had called into the country to battle against the German heretics, were the supports of the Imperial dominion. On the entry of the Prussian army, German patriotism again lifted its head gladly. From the *Gnadenkirchen* rang joyously the praise of the Lord, Who had turned His face from them, and Who now set up a banner for them. Under the protection of the Prussian religious toleration Protestantism soon won back the consciousness of its ecclesiastical superiority, Polish nationality lost ground visibly, and after a few decades the Prussian Silesians stood nearer in thought and customs to their North-German neighbours than to the Silesians on the other side of the frontier.

The Protestant conquerors left the Roman Church in possession of the entire Evangelical Church property, and while England forced the Irish Catholics to support the Anglican State Church by tithes, in Silesia the Protestant had, as before, to pay taxes for the Catholic Church.

---

[1] Churches which Austria allowed the Protestants to build by the treaty of Altranstädt or Friedenskirchen (1707) at Sagan, Freistadt, Militsch, Landeshut, Teschen, and Hirschberg.

Nothing but the traitorous intrigues of the **Roman** clergy during the Seven-Years' War made it necessary for the King to withdraw this excessive indulgence, which led to injustice against the Evangelicals; but even then the Catholic Church remained more favourably placed than in any other Protestant State.

The flourishing condition of the Silesian country under the Prussian sceptre showed sufficiently that the new province had found her natural master, that the crisis in Eastern Germany had terminated irrevocably. Still, the Court of Vienna was undisconcerted and held firmly to the hope of avenging the insult it had suffered, and of pushing down the conqueror of Silesia once more into the motley crowd of German Imperial provinces, like all the other upstart States who before the rebellion had presumed against the Imperial Power. King Frederick knew, too, that the last and crucial clash of arms was still imminent.

During the short years of peace he once tried to exclude the son of Maria Theresa from the Imperial dignity, in order to separate the House of Austria from the Empire for the future. The plan was frustrated by the opposition of the Catholic Courts. The irreconcilable opposition of the two leading powers of Germany decided for a long time ahead the drift of European politics, and drew from the Holy (Roman) Empire the last spurt.

With anxious foreboding, the nation saw another

Thirty-Years' War on the horizon. What had ripened in the quiet work of hard decades appeared to the next generation merely as a wonderful chance, as the happy adventure of an ingenious brain. Outstanding among the diplomatic correspondence of the period is the prophecy of the Dane Bernstorff, who, in the year 1759, wrote sadly to Choiseul: "Everything which you undertake to-day to prevent the rise of an entirely military Monarchy in the middle of Germany, whose iron arm will soon crush the minor princes—is all labour wasted!"

All the neighbouring Powers, both east and west, bore a grudge against the lucky prince who alone had carried off the great prize out of the confusion of the War of the Austrian Succession, and truly, not only the personal hate of mighty women wove at the net of the great conspiracy which threatened to draw together over Frederick's head. Europe felt that the old traditional form of the Balance of Power would totter as soon as the conquering Great Power established itself in the middle of the continent.

The Vatican saw with anxiety how the hated home of the heretics received its liberty again; only through the intervention of Rome was it achieved that those old enemies, the two great Catholic Powers, Austria and France, united in contest against Prussia. Its aim was to perpetuate the impotence of Germany.

By a bold attack the King saved his kingdom

from certain ruin, and when he had for seven terrible years defended his German State on the Rhine and the Pregel, on the Peene and the Riesen Mountains, against foreign and half-foreign armies, and in peace had maintained the integrity of his power down to the last village, Prussia seemed to stand in exactly the same place as it had stood at the beginning of the murderous struggle. He had not won a yard of German soil, half the land lay devastated, the rich results of three generations of peaceful industry were almost annihilated, the unlucky new mark[1] had to begin the work of rehabilitation from the beginning for the fourth time.

Even the King himself could never think without bitterness of those terrible days, when the torture of every disaster which one man can bear, almost beyond human endurance, was heaped on his shoulders; what he suffered then appeared to him as the wantonly malicious mood of a spiteful providence, as a tragedy without justice or termination. For all that, there lurked a colossal achievement in the sequel of the struggle which seemed so unfruitful;—the new order in Germany, which, begun with the foundation of the Prussian power, had stood the severest imaginable test, and had proved an irrevocable necessity. A hundred years before Germany was only able to resist the dominion of the Habsburgs by the struggles of an

[1] The "Neumark" is a part of the Prussian Province of Brandenburg.

entire generation, and then had ignominiously to bribe foreign auxiliaries; now seven years sufficed for the poorest provinces to repulse the attack of a world in arms, and German might alone decided the war, for the sole foreign Power which stood at the side of the King faithlessly betrayed him.[1] Germany's star was again in the ascendant. The text which went up exultingly from all Prussian churches: "They have often oppressed me from my youth up, but they have not overcome me," could be said of Germany.

At the beginning of the second campaign, Frederick had cherished the proud hope of fighting his Pharsalia against the House of Austria, and of dictating peace before the walls of Vienna; at that pregnant moment the birth of a great new civilization in the distant future could be recognized, and an alliance of Prussia with Austria's other rival, with Piedmont, was already attempted.

Then the battle of Kollin threw the King back on his defences: he had to struggle for the existence of his State. His attempt to form an Opposition-Reichstag, a North-German Union to oppose to the Imperial tie, came to nothing through the unconquerable jealousy of the small Courts, and chiefly through the haughty reluctance of the Guelph ally. For the abolition of German dualism, for the rebuilding of the Empire, the hour had not yet come; but through the frightful actuality of this war the ancient and obsolete forms of the

[1] England.

German community were morally annihilated, the last veil torn away from the great lie of the Holy (Roman) Empire.

So far no Kaiser had committed outrages against the Fatherland in such an irresponsible way as this Lorraine augmenter of the Empire, who opened all the gates of Germany to foreign plunderers, delivered up the Netherlands to the Bourbons, and the eastern provinces to the Muscovites. And while the Kaiser trampled on his oath, and forfeited every right of his House to the German crown, at Regensburg the shameless farce of the Reichstag and its criminal anathemas was played. The Reichstag cried to the conqueror of Silesia its *Darnach hat Er, Kurfürst, Sich zu richten* ("According to that he, the Kurfürst, must conform"). The Ambassador of Brandenburg threw the messenger of the illustrious assembly downstairs; the Imperial army gathered together hurriedly under the flag of the Bourbon enemy of the Empire, to scatter at once like chaff in the wind before Seydlitz's squadrons of cavalry. The German nation celebrated with joyous exultation the victor of Rossbach, the rebel against Empire and Emperor.

With this confused satyr-play the great tragedy of the Imperial history was brought indeed to a close; what was left of the old German community scarcely preserved even the semblance of life.

But the conqueror who, in the thunder of battles, had thrown overboard the old theocratic ideas,

Frederick the Great 153

was the protector of Protestantism. Exhausted as the ecclesiastical rivalries appeared to the age of enlightenment, Frederick recognized that the permanency of the Westphalian Peace, the equality of the creeds in the Empire, would not be maintainable when once the two great Catholic Powers triumphed; the common Protestant cause offered him the only handle to force the faint-hearted minor princes into war against Austria.

Watchfully his eye followed the intrigues of the priesthood at the Protestant courts; his authority protected the freedom of the Evangelical Church in Württemberg and Hesse, when the successors to their thrones went over to the Roman faith; and more clearly than he himself, his minor North-German allies recognized the religious significance of the war; in the letters of the Hessian Minister, F. A. von Hardenberg, the allies of Prussia were called simply "the Evangelical provinces," and faithful adherence to the Prussian party was held up as the natural attitude of all the Protestant States of the Empire.

Chanting his Lutheran hymns, the Prussian grenadier went out to battle; the Evangelical soldiers of the Swabian district ran away cursing, because they would not fight against their co-religionists; in the conventicles of the English Dissenters pious preachers prayed for the Maccabeus of Evangelism, the Free-thinker Frederick. The Pope presented the field-marshal of the Empress with a consecrated hat and sword, and every new report of victory from the Prussian camp called up a storm of indignation and fear in the Vatican.

A hundred and twenty years before, the Protestant world had lain at the feet of Rome, as if crushed and destroyed, when the flags of Wallenstein's army waved on the shores of the Baltic, and the Stuarts endeavoured to subject their Parliament to their Roman influences. Now a great Protestant Power gave the last blow to the Holy (Roman) Empire, and through the wars on the Ohio and the Ganges it was decided once for all that sea and colonial power should belong to the Protestant and Germanic races.

The struggle for Prussia's existence was the first European war; it created the unity of the new association of States, and gave it the aristocratic form of the Pentarchy. When the new great Central-European Power extorted the recognition of the neighbouring Powers, the two old political systems of the east and west melted into one inseparable community; and at the same time the less powerful States, which occasionally before, through their entering into a coalition, had turned the scale in a great battle, but now could no longer meet the heavy demands of the new grandiose scale of war, sank in position.

The States of the second rank decided to leave the control of European affairs to the great naval and military Powers for the future. Among these five leading Powers were two Protestant and one schismatic; that Europe should fall back under the domination of the Crowned Priest (the Pope) was unthinkable from now on. The establishment of the great German Protestant Power was the heaviest defeat which the Roman Curia had suffered since the appearance of Martin Luther; King Frederick had truly, as the English Ambassador Mitchell said, fought for the freedom of the human race.

From the school of sufferings and struggles there sprang for the Prussian people a living sense of nationality: it justified the King in talking of his *nation Prussienne*. To be a Prussian had up to this been a stern duty: it was now an honour.

The thought of the State, the Fatherland, forced its way, exciting and nerving, into millions of hearts; even the crushed soul of the poor felt a breath of the antique sense of citizenship which emanated from the simple words of the King: "It is not necessary that I should live, but very necessary that I should do my duty and fight for my Fatherland." Everywhere in Prussia, under the stiff forms of an absolute monarchy, stirred the spirit of sacrifice and the great passion of the national war.

The army which had been victorious in Frederick's last battles was national; recruiting in foreign countries was in the nature of things impossible in the catastrophes of the period. The provincial estates voluntarily equipped those regiments which had saved the fortresses of Magdeburg, Stettin, and Küstrin for the State; the Pomeranian seamen banded together to defend with their small navy the mouths of the Oder against the Swedes. For six years the officials, poor as church-mice, received no pay, and yet quietly discharged their duties as if it were an understood thing.

Emulously all the provinces rivalled each other in carrying out their "damned duty," as the Prussian phrase ran (*ihre verfluchte Pflicht und Schuldigkeit*); from the gallant peasant of the Rhenish county of Mörs to the unhappy East-Prussians, who with quiet tenacious opposition had stood firm against the Russian conqueror, and would not be disturbed in their determined faithfulness when the inexorable King accused them of falling-off and overwhelmed them with manifestations of his displeasure.

The educational power of war awakened again in these North-German races above all that rough pride, which once inspirited the invaders of Italy (*Romfahrer*) and the conquerors of the Slavs in the Middle Ages. The alert self-reliance of the Prussians contrasted strongly with the inoffensive, kindly modesty of the other Germans. Graf Hertzberg confidently refuted the doctrine of Montesquieu on the virtues of republicanism: where in republicanism had there flourished a stauncher public spirit than here, under the bracing northern sky, among the descendants of those heroic nations, the Vandals and the Goths, who had once shattered the Roman Empire? The same spirit existed in the mass of the people; it was betrayed now in confident bragging, in the thousand satirical anecdotes of Austrian stupidity and Prussian Hussar strategies current, now in pathetic stories of conscientious fidelity.

The young sailor Joachim Nettelbeck comes to Danzig, and is hired to row the King of Poland across the harbour; someone claps a hat on his head with the monogram of King Augustus; for a long time he resists, for it seems to him a betrayal of his Prussian King to wear the badge of a foreign sovereign; at last he has to submit, but the earned ducat burns in his hand, and as soon as he gets home to Pomerania he presents the ill-gotten money to the first Prussian invalid who crosses his path. So susceptible has the political pride in this nation become, which a few decades before was demoralized by its domestic troubles.

It was not to be forgotten that to the two great princes of war, to Cæsar and Alexander, from now onwards a Prussian was associated as third. In the character of the North-German, united to a tough perseverance, there is a strain of high-spirited light-heartedness, which loves to play with danger, and the Prussians found this characteristic of theirs again in the General Frederick, raised to the pitch of genius: when he, after a hard apprenticeship, ripened rapidly into the master, threw aside the cautious rules of the old ponderous science of war, and even to the enemy "dictated the precepts of war," being always ready to seek the decision in open battle; when he again raised the sharpest weapon, cavalry, to that place which was due to it in great battles; when he after every victory, and after each of his three defeats, always maintained anew "the prerogative of the initiative."

The successful results show how well the King and his people understood one another. A close circle of heroes gathered round the chief or King, and spread down to the lowest rank of the army that gay love of daring, that spirit of the offensive, which has remained the strength of the Prussian army in all its great periods.

From the provincial nobles and Pomeranian peasants Frederick drew the feared Ansbach-Baireuth Dragoons and the Zieten Hussars, who soon surpassed the wild-riding races of Hungary in their mad dash and their spirited charges. With pride the King said that with such soldiers there was no risk: "A general who in other armies would be considered foolhardy, is considered by us only as doing his duty!" The twelve campaigns of the Frederician period have given the Prussian people and army the martial spirit as their characteristic spirit for ever. Even to-day, when the conversation turns to war the North-German falls involuntarily into the expressions of those heroic days, and speaks, as did Frederick, of "brilliant campaigns" and "fulminant attacks."

The good-hearted kindliness of the Germans

outside Prussia needed a long time to overcome its aversion to the hard realism of this Frederician theory, which so ungenerously attacked its enemy when it was least welcome. But when the great year of 1757 swept over the German nation, when victorious attack and heavy defeat, new daring recovery and new glowing victory crowded in bewildering haste, and when always from the wild flight of events stood out the picture of the King, uniformly great and commanding, the people felt themselves gripped heart and soul, and were staggered at this vision of sheer human greatness.

The hard, weather-beaten figure of old Fritz, as the blows of an inexorable Fate had forged it, exercised its irresistible witchery on countless faithful souls, who had regarded the dazzling figure of the youthful Hero of Hohenfriedberg only with awe. The Germans were, as Goethe said of his Frankfurters, Fritz-mad (*Fritzishgesinnt*)—"For what did Prussia matter to us?"—and watched with bated breath as the untamable man, year-out, year-in, warded off destruction. That overwhelming union of unmixed joy and love which occasionally illuminates the history of happier nations with a golden light, was, it is true, still denied to rent Germany.

As Luther and Gustavus Adolphus, the only two heroes before that whose pictures had impressed themselves indelibly on the hearts of our nation, so Frederick was feared in the episcopal lands[1] of the Rhine and the Main as the great enemy. But the vast majority of Protestants, and wide circles of the Catholic people, and, above all, certain leaders of the new learning and poetry, followed him with warm sympathy; people caught at his witticisms, and told marvel after marvel of his grenadiers and hussars. The heart of the previously so humble race swelled at the thought that the first man of the century was ours, that the fame of the King sounded as far as Morocco and America.

So far few knew that the Prussian battle-fame was only the ancient military glory of the German nation come to light again; even Lessing occasionally spoke of the Prussians as of a half-foreign nation, and remarked with astonishment that heroism seemed as born in them as in the Spartans. Gradually even the masses began to feel that Frederick fought for Germany. The battle of Rossbach, the *bataille en douceur*, as he called it mockingly, was the richest in results for our national life of his victories.

If in this domesticated race there still lived a political emotion, it was a silent animosity against French arrogance, which, so often chastised with the German sword, had always in the end remained in possession of the field, and was once again covering the Rhine-lands with blood and ruin. Now Frederick's good sword met it, and struck it down in a pool of shame; a shout of exultation

[1] In German, crooked-staff lands (*Krummstabslande*).

rang through all the German provinces, and the Swabian Schubart cried: *Da griff ich ungestüm die goldene Harfe, darein zu stürmen Friedrichs Lob* ("Impetuously I seize the golden harp, to make it storm Frederick's praise").

For the first time in history the Germans in the Empire succumbed to a feeling like national pride, and they sang with old Gleim: *Lasst uns Deutsche sein und bleiben!* ("Let us be and remain Germans.") The French officers returning from the German battle-fields proclaimed naïvely in Paris itself the praise of the victor of Rossbach, since their pride could not yet imagine it possible that this little Prussia could ever seriously threaten the power of France; in German comedies, however, the once-feared Frenchman now filled the rôle either of the butt or the vain adventurer.

A political understanding of the character of the Prussian State had not, it is true, come to the nation even yet; this learned people lived in a wonderful ignorance of the deciding factors of its modern history as well as of the institutions of its mightiest State-organization.

If the victories of Frederick had somewhat appeased the old hatred against Prussia, even in the Protestant provinces of the Empire every citizen congratulated himself if he was not a Prussian. The industrious fictions of the Austrian party found willing listeners everywhere. "This free people," Frederick Nicolai wrote in the year

1780 from Swabia, "look down on us poor Brandenburgers as slaves."

The force of the mighty State appealed only to strong and ambitious natures. From the beginning of the Frederician period a distinguished phalanx of the brilliant young men of the Empire had begun to enter into the Prussian service; some were impelled by their amazement at the King, others by the longing for exuberant activity, and some had a vague presentiment of the destinies of this Monarchy.

It had now fully outgrown the narrow-mindedness of provincial life and spontaneously absorbed all the healthy elements in the Empire, and found in the ranks of the immigrants many of her most faithful and capable servants, also her deliverer, the Freiherr Karl von Stein.

With the Peace of Hubertusburg there dawned for the North-Germans four decades of deep peace; that richly blessed time of peace, of which old Goethe afterwards thought so often with gratitude.

At that time the old tradition of Prussia's poverty gradually became a fable. Social life, particularly in the capital, took on richer and freer forms, the national prosperity received a surprising impetus, German poetry entered on her great period. The war had at once simplified and rendered more difficult the position of the Empire. Of the old order there was nothing left but the still unsolved opposition of the two Great Powers. A presentiment of a difficult decision went through the German world; the minor Courts discussed in energetic conferences as to how they should protect themselves by forming an alliance of the minor Powers, in case another encounter of the "two German Colossi" threaten to crush them. But King Frederick, thoroughly aware of the infinite power of the inertia in this old Empire, resigned himself to recuperating the exhausted strength of his own State; his German policy for the future had for its only aim to keep out of the Empire every influence of foreign Powers and to balance the power of Austria.

A great danger which threatened the German Power from the east snatched him from his peaceful plans. The Polish Republic had been since the war subject to the will of the Czarina; the formal union of the shattered State with the Russian Empire appeared to be only a question of time.

Then the idea of the division of Poland, which crossed the designs of the Russians and set boundaries to their ambitions, dawned on Frederick. It was a victory of German policy, at once over the grabbing land-greed of Russia, and over the Western Powers, who were pushed aside regardlessly by the boldly advancing Powers of the East.

The necessary act, it is true, opened up to view immeasurable complications, since the decayed Empire of the Sarmatian aristocracy was now irretrievably approaching its downfall; but it was necessary, it saved faithful East Prussia from the return of Muscovite government, and ensured for the State the bridge between the lands of the Pregel and the Oder, which the Crown-Prince Frederick had already recognized as indispensable. The King appeared for the second time as the increaser of the Empire; he gave back again to the Greater Fatherland the stronghold of the dominions of the Teutonic order, the lovely Weichsel valley, which in days of yore the German knight wrested from the barbarians, the German peasant from the wrath of the elements.

When the provinces of West Prussia "swore allegiance to the restored government"—as the festival medal of the oath of allegiance says significantly—in the refectory of the Grand Master's castle at Marienburg, the outrages upon this German land, three hundred years ago, from the arrogance of the Poles and the treachery of the provincial authorities, were expiated. The five hundred years' war between the Germans and the Poles for the possession of the Baltic coast was decided in favour of Germany.

Then the State, itself still bleeding from the wounds of the last war, began the hard work of peaceful re-conquest. The Sarmatian nobility had committed horrible outrages in the Weichsel district, with that insolent disregard of the rights of others and the nationality of others which distinguishes the Poles above all the nations of Europe.

The new sovereign had to rule with more vigour

than before in Silesia to bring the German character back to honour in the famous old cities of German glory and industry, in Thorn, Culm, and Marienburg, and to introduce again the rudiments of agriculture in the devastated land. And as once the first German conquerors wrested corn-lands from the marshes, so now out of the swamps, near the rising town of Bromberg, rose the busy Netze district, the creation of the second conqueror.

Frederick himself surmised only vaguely what the re-acquisition of the country of the Teutonic Knights meant in the great continuity of German history; but the nation had become quite unfamiliar with their own history—they scarcely knew that these districts had once been German. Some cursed with the harsh arrogance of a censor the ambiguous diplomatic moves which had paved the way for the partition of the country; others repeated credulously what Poland's old confederates, the French, invented to stigmatize the partitioning Powers; the majority remained cold, and fortified themselves anew with the current idea that old Fritz had the devil in him (*dass der alte Fritz den Teufel im Leib habe*). For the new benefit which he had conferred on our people, not one person in the Empire thanked him.

The restless ambition of Kaiser Joseph II led the King back at the eve of his life to the idea of the Imperial policy which occupied his youth. The Court of Vienna gave up the appearance of Conservatism, which alone could ensure for the

Kaiser-House respect in the Empire, and endeavoured to compensate itself for the loss of Silesia in Bavaria. The whole course of Austrian history for two hundred years, the continually growing separation between the Imperial State and the Empire, was to be pulled up all at once by an adventurous invasion. Then King Frederick for the second time concluded his alliance with the Wittelsbachs, and with the sword prohibited the House of Austria from extending its power on German soil; more sharply and clearly than ever before the opposition of the two rivals came to light.

The War of the Bavarian Succession showed in its plan of campaign, as in its political aims, surprising resemblances to the deciding war of 1866, but Prussia did not draw the sword to free Germany from the dominion of Austria, as it did three generations later, but only to ward off Austrian encroachments and for the preservation of the *status quo*. Although the ageing hero no longer possessed the dash to carry out his plan of campaign on so large a scale as he had planned, Prussia's power proved itself strong enough to force the Court of Vienna to yield without any glowing military success. Bavaria was saved for the second time; the arrogant Imperial Court had to submit to "plead before the Tribunal of Berlin," and the embittered Prince Kaunitz made that prophecy which was to be fulfilled on the field of Königgrätz, although not in the sense that the prophet meant, that if ever the swords of Austria and Prussia clashed together again, they would not be returned to their sheaths until "the decision had fallen definitely, completely, and irrevocably."

Almost more valuable than the immediate result was the enormous revulsion of opinion in the Empire. The dreaded disturber of peace, the rebel against Emperor and Empire, now appeared to the nation as the wise shelterer of right; the small Courts, which had so often trembled before the Prussian sword, scared by Kaiser Joseph's restless plans, looked for help to the arbitrator at Sans Souci. In the peasant farms of the Bavarian Alps hung the picture of the old man with his three-cornered hat beside the national (Bavarian) Saint Corbinian. In the chorus of Swabian and North-German poets, who told of the fame of the King, mingled already isolated voices of the deeply hostile electorate of Saxony; the bard Ringulph sang in enraptured odes how "from the breast of the Almighty, King Frederick, your great battle-lusting spirit came."

Only a short while before had K. F. Moser avowed that the vision of man was not capable of following this eagle in its loftiness, that perhaps hereafter there would appear a Newton of political science, capable of measuring the orbit of the Frederician policy. But now the Germans began to feel that this mysterious policy was wonderfully simple at bottom, that the Statesman Frederick, divested of every hatred, every love, quasi-im-personal, always desired only what the clearly recognized position of his State demanded.

When the rebellion broke out in North America, and the civilized world hailed the new sun which was rising in the West, Frederick did not conceal his joy. His own youthful Great Power was a new State, which had entered the circle of the old Powers with welcome; it did him good to see England, which had so shamefully betrayed him in the last war, and had then impeded him during the Polish negotiations in the acquisition of Danzig, now in painful embarrassment. He declared openly that he would not defend Hanover for ungrateful England a second time: he even once forbade the passage through his dominions of the English mercenaries, bought in Germany, because he was revolted by this sordid traffic in human beings, and still more because he needed the young men of the Empire for his own army.

He made use of the distress of the Ocean-Queen to preserve the naval rights of the smaller Powers by an alliance of armed neutrality; after the peace, he, first among the European princes, concluded a commercial treaty with the young Republic, and in it acknowledged that free, human comprehension of international law which has since then remained a faithfully preserved tradition of the Prussian State. But neither his hate of the "God-damn Government," nor the boundless popularity which saluted him in the (American) colonies, ever moved him to go one step beyond the interests of his State. His old enemy Kaunitz still could explain the proud course of the Frederician policy only as springing from the immeasurable cunning of a demoniacal nature.

But in the Empire the old mistrust gradually disappeared; its people observed that nowhere were their affairs weighed so soberly, so exactly, so watchfully, and so coldly as in the hermitage of Sans Souci.

So the impossible happened—the high nobility of the Empire gathered round Frederick's flag of its own free will. Kaiser Joseph resumed his Bavarian plans—to shatter Prussia's power, as he himself admitted. He at the same time threatened the stability of his ecclesiastical neighbours with rash thoughts of secularization. A sudden terror gripped the small States when they saw their natural protector become an enemy; an alliance of the Central Powers was discussed, a league of the ecclesiastical princes, until at last the acknowledgment was forced that nothing could be done without Prussia's help.

With youthful zeal the old King entered into the quarrel. All the alluring proposals which were put forward that he should share the possession of Germany with the Emperor he rejected as bait for "the common greed." He conquered his contempt for the minor princes, and realized that only through strict justice could he attach these people to himself. He succeeded in winning the great majority of the electors, and most of the more powerful princes, for his German Princes' Bund, and in maintaining the old Imperial Constitutions and the *status quo* of the Imperial States against the Kaiser.

"Only the love of my Fatherland, and the duty of a good citizen," he wrote, "drive me at my age to this undertaking." What he had dreamt in his youth had an even more brilliant fulfilment for the patriarch: no longer hidden behind a Bavarian shadow-Emperor, as in the Silesian wars, but in the face of the whole world, the King of Prussia now came into the arena as the protector of Germany. All the neighbouring Powers, who counted on Germany's weakness, saw the unexpected turn of the Imperial policy with grave anxiety. France and Russia approached the Court of Vienna; the Alliance of 1756 bade fair to be renewed. The Turin Cabinet, on the contrary, hailed the Princes' Bund with joy as "the tutelary god of the Italian States."

For two hundred years the policy of federalism in the Empire had not got beyond a half start; but now that it leaned on the power of Prussia it suddenly won a large following. The memory of the times of Maximilian I and the Elector Berthold's attempts at reform rose again to the surface. The Princes' Bund was formed to uphold the Imperial theocratic Germany. But if it lasted, if Prussia maintained her position of leader at the head of the great Imperial States, the old forms of the Imperial Diet had to lose their meaning; the prospect was opened up of shattering the Austrian system to its foundations, and as Graf Hertzberg joyfully proclaimed, of excluding the Archdukes from the great German institutions, of transferring the Imperial Crown to another house at the next election, and of placing the guidance of the Empire in the hands of the most powerful States.

The young Karl August of Weimar proposed to submit the old privileges which ensured the House of Austria its unique position to an Imperial test. It almost seemed as if the great problem of Germany's future would be solved in peace. But the Princes' Bund could not last; and this bitter truth was hidden least of all from the common-sensible mind of the old King. Only a series of chance circumstances, only the defection of Kaiser Joseph from the old approved traditions of Austrian statecraft, had scared the minor princes into Frederick's arms; their trust of Prussia went no further than their fear of Austria. With the utmost reluctance the Electorate of Saxony submitted to the guidance of the younger and less aristocratic House of Brandenburg; Hanover showed itself hardly less mistrustful; even the humblest and weakest of the allied States, Weimar and Dessau, secretly discussed, so Goethe tells us, how they could protect themselves against their Prussian protector's lust of power.

As soon as the Hofburg (the Court of Vienna) dropped their covetous plans, the old natural formation of parties must revive; the ecclesiastical princes, who now sought help in Berlin, could see in Protestant Prussia only the sworn enemy of their authority. Since Frederick knew this, since he penetrated his faithful confederates to the very marrow with his piercing gaze, he did not let himself be deceived by the success of the minute into imagining that this Schmalkaldic League was anything but a makeshift, a means of preserving the momentary balance. Karl August, in large-hearted enthusiasm, sketched bold plans for the building-up of the new Imperial Association; he thought of a customs' union, of military conventions, of a German code; Johannes Müller extolled the Princes' Bund in the most high-flown pamphlets, Schubart in stirring lyrical effusions, and Dohm concluded a clever pamphlet with these words: "German and Prussian interests can never stand in one another's way." The discerning mind of the old King was not moved by such dreams; he knew that only a colossal war could break the power of Austria in the Empire; it sufficed him to keep it within the bounds of justice, because he needed peace for his country.

For a serious reform of the Empire there were still lacking all the preliminary conditions; there was lacking, above all, the will of the nation. Even the Imperialist defenders of the Princes' Bund could not get beyond the old chimera of German freedom. The Josephin policy, so Hertzberg stirringly protested, threatened to agglomerate the powers of Germany into a mass, to subject free Europe to a universal monarchy; and in Dohm's eyes it appears as a praiseworthy aim of the new Bund to keep open the western borders of Austria, so that France can stride into it at any time on behalf of German freedom.

The nation realized dimly that the existing conditions were not worthy to exist; in Schubart's writings the small Swabian territories are often described as an open dove-cot, which lay close to the claws of the royal weasel. But all these ideas and presentiments were held under by a feeling of hopeless resignation which modern energy can hardly understand; the Germans felt as if an inscrutable Providence had condemned this people to continue for all eternity in an abnormal State which had long lost every right to exist.

When the great King departed, it is true, he left behind a generation which looked on the world more joyfully and proudly than its fathers, and enormously had the State power which might in the future bring Germany a new day been raised. But the question: By what ways and means could a vital scheme for the German community be created? appeared at Frederick's death still almost as problematical as it had been at his ascension to the throne; indeed, it had not once been seriously raised by the great majority of Germans. The first beginnings of a formation of parties in the nation scarcely existed; it seemed as if only a miracle from heaven could help the helpless. The terrible confusion of the situation was shown with sinister clearness by the one fact, that the hero who with his good sword had once proved the futility of the institutions of the Empire had come himself to defend these lifeless forms against the head of the Empire.

If Frederick could only prepare, and not complete, the settlement of the German constitution, he had, on the other hand, deeply and lastingly influenced the inner policy of the German territories, and brought our nation to a nobler public spirit and a worthier view of the character of the State. He stood at the end of the great days of unlimited monarchy, and yet appeared to his contemporaries as the representative of a new conception of the State, an enlightened despotism.

Only genius possesses the strength for propaganda, is capable of gathering the resisting world round the banner of new ideas. As the ideas of the Revolution were first circulated effectively by Napoleon, so was that serious comprehension of the duties of the kingdom which governed the Prussian throne from the time of the Great Elector first transferred to the consciousness of the people by Frederick. Only after the brilliant successes of the Silesian wars was the gaze of the world, which so far had hung wonderingly on the magnificence of the Court of Versailles, turned seriously to the unostentatious crown of the Hohenzollerns.

In war and in his foreign policy the King showed the incomparable creative power of his genius; in the inner administration he was the son of his father. He invigorated the traditional forms of the State with the strength of genius, developed the free and incomplete in a free and comprehensive spirit; he did not undertake to erect anything new. And yet he knew how to unite the idea of a political kingdom, which his father, as a firm, practical man, had realized, with the civilizing influences of the century; incessantly he gave himself and others an account of his doings. Already as Crown-Prince he had won a place among the political thinkers of the age; his Anti-Machiavellism remains, in spite of all the weakness of immaturity, surely the best and deepest exposition of the duties of the princely office in an absolute monarchy which was ever penned. Afterwards, in the first years of the joy of conquest, he wrote the *Fürstenspiegel* ("Mirror for Princes") for the young Duke of Württemberg; but louder than all theories spoke his actions, as he proved his words in the days of trial, and showed the world what it meant "to think, live, and die as a King."

Lastly, Providence showed him that favour which even genius needs, if it is to impress its seal on a whole age: the good fortune of adequately living up to his gifts until a ripe old age. He was now the Nestor, the recognized first man of the European princes. His fame raised the prestige of all thrones; from his words and deeds other Kings learned to think highly of their vocation.

The old-established conception of the minor princes, that the land and the people belonged to the Most Serene Princely House, lost ground after Frederick drily observed: "The Sovereign has no nearer relation than his State, whose interests must always stand before the ties of blood."

The dynastic overweening conceit of the Bourbons showed up in its futility when he, on his ascension to the throne, turned his back to the light pleasures of life with the words: "My duty is my only god," and then for half a century served this one god with all his strength, and to the thanks of his people gave always the deliberate answer: "For that I am here." With such secular impartiality no crowned head had ever spoken of the princely dignity as this autocrat, who unhesitatingly recognized the right of a Republic as of a parliamentary kingdom, and sought the greatness of absolute monarchy only in the arduousness of its duties: "The Prince should belong to the State head and heart; he is the Pope of the Civil Religion of the State."

The new generation of the high nobility fashioned itself by Frederick's example and the social ideas of the new civilization. The small sultans who raged in the time of Frederick William I were followed by a long succession of well-meaning, dutiful fathers of their peoples, such as Charles Frederick of Baden and Frederick Christian of Saxony.

Already it often happened that, in the Prussian fashion, the princes had a military education; Christian toleration, the advancement of schools, and the well-being of his people, were considered princely duties; individual minor States, like Brunswick, granted to the Press even greater freedom than Prussia itself. Even in certain ecclesiastical districts there was a change for the better; the Münster district extolled the mild and careful administration of Fürstenberg.[1]

Of course, it was not everywhere, and at one blow, that the deeply rooted offences of minor-princely despotism disappeared; the old bad practice of selling soldiers now, during the American war, reached the summit of its infamy, and showed what the German princes were capable of. The Frederician system of benevolent absolutism for the benefit of the people often led in the narrow spheres of the minor States to empty sport, or to oppressive guardianship. The Margrave of Baden called his exchequer shortly: "the natural trustee of our subjects"; many a well-meaning minor prince abused his dominions by the new-fangled physiocratic system of taxation, by all sorts of unripe philanthropic experiments, and the Oettingen-Oettingen-*Landesdirektorium* had to give the inquisitive reigning prince an accurate account of the "names, breed, use, and external appearance" of the collective dogs to be found in princely lands, besides "additional, unpresuming, most humble advice."

[1] There is a noble Westphalian family called Fürstenberg, one of whom was Prince-Bishop of Münster about this time, who effected important reforms in the administration.

But, on the whole, the generation of princes of those eighty years formed the most honourable which had sat on German thrones for a long time. Wherever he could, the King opposed the excesses of his compeers, freed old Moser from prison, and ensured the Württembergers the continuance of their constitution. The Empire as a whole lay hopeless, but in many of its members a new hopeful life was pulsing.

And far beyond Germany's borders the example of Frederick carried influence. Maria Theresa became his most docile pupil; she spread the idea of the Frederician monarchy in the Catholic world. Surrounded by weak neighbours, old Austria had so far lived on careless and sleepy; only the strengthening of her ambitious rival in the north forced the Imperial State to exert her powers boldly. The North-German Haugwitz fashioned the administration of Austria, as far as was possible, according to the Prussian pattern, and from these Austrian reforms, in turn, came the enlightened despotism which from now on began its impetuous, violent attempts at a millennium in all Latin countries, in Naples and Tuscany, in Spain and Portugal.

The pride of the Bourbons stood out longest against the new conception of the monarchy; at Versailles, with jeering smiles, it was told how at the Court of Potsdam the lord-high-chamberlain had never yet handed the King his shirt. Only when it was too late, when the forces of the

Revolution were already knocking at the doors, did the French Court begin to surmise something of the duties of the kingdom.

The Crown of the Bourbons never wholly emerged from the dull atmosphere of smug self-adulation and contempt of the people; therefore it collapsed shamefully. But among the Germans the spirit of monarchism, which lay in the blood of our people, and even in the centuries of polycracy was never wholly lost, was strengthened anew by King Frederick. In no other nation of modern history has a kingship had such a large and high-minded view of its problems; therefore the German people remained, even when the time of the Parliamentary struggles came, the most faithful of the great civilized peoples to the idea of monarchy.

The love of peace of the House of Hohenzollern remained alive even in its greatest war-princes. Frederick valued power, but only as a means for the well-being and civilization of the nations; that it should be an end in itself, that the struggle for power as such should bestow historic fame, seemed to him as an insult to the honour of a sovereign. Therefore he wrote his passionate polemic treatise against Machiavelli. Therefore, in his writings, he returned again and again to the terrible warning of Charles XII of Sweden.

He might have felt secretly that in his own breast were working irresistible forces which might lead him to similar errors; and he was never tired of portraying the hollowness of objectless military fame, and had the bust of the King of Sweden contemptuously erected beneath the feet of the Muse in the round hall at Sans Souci.

Already in his impetuous youth he had made up his mind about the moral objects of power.

This State must become strong [he wrote at that time], that it may play the lofty rôle of preserving peace only from love of justice, and not from fear. But if ever injustice, bias, and vice gain the upper hand in Prussia, then I wish the House of Brandenburg a speedy downfall. That says all.

When at the end of the Seven-Years' War he felt strong enough to preserve peace out of justice, then he turned his attention to the restoration of the national prosperity with such zeal that the army was actually injured.

It is a fact: the general who had overwhelmed the Flag of Prussia with laurels left the army in a worse condition than he had found it on his ascension to the throne; he could not approach his father as a military organizer. He needed the industrial population for his devastated country, and therefore patronized on principle the enlisting of troops for his army in foreign countries. The regimental commanders were to draw up the register of their recruiting-districts in agreement with the *Landräte* (sheriffs) and surveyors of taxes.

From that time there occurred in every district

each year that struggle between the military claims and the civil interests which, afterward, in changing forms, occurred again and again in Prussian history. This time the struggle was decided in favour of political economy. The civil authorities sought to preserve every man who was in any way capable or well-to-do from the red cantonal collar. The King himself interfered to help, and freed from compulsory service numerous classes of the population—the new immigrants, the families of all traders and manufacturers, the household servants of landowners. Many cities—nay, whole provinces, as Ostfriesland—obtained privileges. Soon after the peace the majority of the army consisted of foreigners.

Frederick thought highly of the army, and liked to call it the Atlas who carried this State on his strong shoulders; the military fame of the seven years had an after-effect; the service of the common soldier, it is true, was counted in Prussia, as everywhere else in the world, as a misfortune, but not as a disgrace, as it was in the rest of the Empire. The King brought the great summer manœuvres on the Mockerauer Heath to a technical completeness which the art of manœuvres has probably never reached since then. He was never tired of impressing on his officers "to love the detail, which also has its distinction," and wrote for their instruction his military handbook, the most mature of all his works.

Not one improvement in military affairs escaped

him; at a great age he yet adopted a new arm of the service, the light infantry, the green Fusiliers according to the pattern of the American riflemen. The fame of the Potsdamer parade-ground drew spectators from all countries. In Turin Victor Amadeus and his generals faithfully copied every movement of the great Prussian drill-sergeant down to the bent carriage of the head; and when the young Lieutenant Gneisenau saw the pointed helmets of the grenadiers on parade glittering in the sun, he cried enthusiastically: "Say, which of all nations could well copy this marvellous sight?"

In spite of that, in Frederick's last years the army sank undoubtedly. The flower of the old officers' corps lay on the battle-fields; during the seven years—an unprecedented occurrence in the history of war—all the renowned generals, with scanty exceptions, were left on the field or were disabled; their successors had known war only in subalterns' positions, and looked for the secret of the Frederician conquests only in the mechanical exercises of the parade-ground. Among the foreign officers were many doubtful adventurers who only courted favour; for the proud frankness of a York or a Blücher there was no more room.

The King, less friendly to the *bourgeoisie* than his father, believed that only the aristocracy had a sense of honour, and dismissed the bourgeois officers from the majority of the regiments. In the noble officers' corps there arose an aristocratic arrogance (*Junkersinn*), which soon became more intolerable to the people than the coarse roughness of earlier times. The old hired soldiers lived in the end comfortably with wife and child, in civil employment, and abominated war for a country which had always remained foreign to them. Frederick had already noticed with astonishment in the war of the Bavarian Succession how little this army accomplished; the reason for the deterioration he did not penetrate. The Eudæmonism of his age made it impossible for him to recognize the moral forces which swayed the army. He had once, after the custom of the period, formed Prussian regiments from Austrian and Saxon prisoners of war, and could not even learn by the desertions *en masse* of these unfortunate men; he had in the last years of the war sufficiently experienced what an army of his own people was capable of, yet such forcible calling out of the entire national strength always remained to him only an expedient for desperate days, "when the defence of the Fatherland and an imminent danger depends on it."

Of his statesmen, Hertzberg alone had religiously observed the daring ideas of Frederick William I; he wanted to gradually purge the army of all foreigners. "Then we shall be as unconquerable as the Greeks and the Romans!" But the old King saw with satisfaction how his unfortunate land was being strengthened agriculturally, and now defined the ideal of the army with the astounding words: "The peaceful citizen shall not even notice when the nation is at war." So one of the pillars which upheld the edifice of State—universal service—began slowly to totter.

The traditional class-system of the estates of the realm and the organization of government dependent from it the King upheld more strictly than his father; he helped with instruction and ruthless coercion, with gifts and loans, as often as the rôle which was prescribed for the peasant, the citizen, or the nobleman in the household of the nation no longer seemed to suffice him.

The nobility was to remain the first rank in the State, since "I need them for my army and my civil administration." By the mortgage institutions, and by considerable support with ready money, Frederick attained the conservation of the large estates of the nobles after the devastation of the years of war. Therefore he made as little attempt as his father to abolish the serfdom of the peasants, which was so repugnant to his magnanimity. By the common law, it is true, the harsher forms of serfdom were done away with, but there still remained the somewhat less oppressive hereditary rights of the dynasty. The Government contented itself with modifying the harshness of the existing lordship.

Unnoticed and undesired by the older princes, in the meantime there began a displacement of the conditions of social power, which was rich in results. The new literature drew an educated public from all classes; the merchants and tradespeople of the great cities, the simple tenants of the enlarged dominions of the monarchy, gradually attained to an assured position and to a conviction that the privileges of the nobility could not endure much longer. The nobility lost by degrees the moral as well as the economic foundations of their rank. The structure of the old class-organization was imperceptibly undermined.

The administrative arrangements of the father remained unchanged under the son, except that he added to the provincial departments of the *General Direktorium* four new ones, embracing the entire State, for the administration of War, Mercantile Policy, Mining Matters, and Forestry, and thus made another step on the way to a united State. The Crown still stood high above the people. *Gensdarmes* had to force the peasants to use the seed-potatoes presented by the King; the command of the Sheriff (*Landrat*) and the Board enforced against the tenacious passive opposition of the parties concerned communal drainage and other enterprises, and all improvements of agricultural appliances. The wholly exhausted energies of the people for civil industries could only be reawakened by a violent system of protection.

The flaws of the Frederician political economy were not due to the eternal and well-meant interference of the supreme power, which the age had in no way outlived, but in the fiscal deceptions which the King was compelled to resort to through the embarrassments of his affairs; he had to use fully three quarters of his revenue for the army, and sought to make up what was necessary for his administration by monopolies and indirect taxes. The finances in their clumsiness resembled those of a large private household. Almost half the regular revenues came from the Crown lands and forests; only this rich property of the State rendered his high expenditure possible; it served at the same time for the technical education of the peasants. The amount of the principal taxes was fixed by statute; the movable revenue of the administration had to be drawn on for the extraordinary expenses of settling people on the soil and cultivating.

The carefully accumulated treasure sufficed for several short campaigns; but old Prussia could not carry on a long severe war without a foreign subsidy, since the laws of the *Landtag*, the traditional views of the bureaucracy, and the crude financial system, forbade every loan. Strong as was the growth of the wealth and well-being of the middle-classes, the greater advance of the more fortunate neighbouring peoples was not easily caught up. The Prussian State still remained the poorest of the Great Powers of the West; essentially an agricultural land, it played a modest rôle in international commerce, even after Frederick had opened up an avenue to the North Sea by the conquest of Ostfriesland; for the mouth of the Ems, like the mouth of the Oder, had no rich industrial *Hinterland*.

As a reformer, Frederick was effective only in those spheres of the inner affairs of the State which his predecessor had not understood. He created the new Prussian Bench of Judges, as his father formed the modern German Bureaucracy. He knew that the administration of justice is a political function, which is inseparably connected with the State; he made all his dominions independent of the Imperial High Court of Justice, forbade the introduction of the interpretations of the Faculty of Jurists, created a Ministry of Justice in addition to the *General Direktorium*, gave the entire administration of justice into the hands of a hierarchically organized State Bureaucracy, which itself educated its rising generation, and took under strict superintendence that private (or independent) jurisdiction which still continued to exist in some minor departments.

The absolute independence of the courts of justice in relation to the Administration was solemnly promised, and kept inviolably, with the exception of a few cases of well-meaning despotic high-handed justice. The new Bench preserved in a modest domestic position an honourable class-feeling, and while the Imperial courts were full of corruption, the proud saying was coined in Prussia, and that against the King: *Il y a des juges à Berlin.* The desire often obtruded itself upon the friend of Enlightenment, to whom the

State was the work of the conscious human will, that not an inherited and traditional law but a law founded on experience, such as was generally desired, must reign in the State; all his life Frederick cherished the idea of carrying out the first comprehensive codification of the law which had been attempted since the time of Justinian.

Only after his death did the *Allgemeine Landrecht*[1] come in force, which shows more clearly than any other work of the epoch the double-sidedness of the Frederician conception of the State. On the one side, the code preserved the traditional social distinctions so carefully that the entire legal system had to accommodate itself to the class organization, and even—against the common law—the nobility were granted special marriage laws, and on the other it carried the idea of the sovereignty of the State to its logical conclusion with such daring, that many a passage anticipated the ideas of the French Revolution, which made Mirabeau say that with these ideas Prussia hurried on a century ahead of the rest of Europe.

The aim of the State is the general well-being, and only for the sake of this end may the State limit the natural freedom of the citizens—and repeal any existing privilege. The King is only the head of the State, and has duties and rights only as such—and this in the days when Biener and other renowned lawyers were fighting for the privileges and rights of the German princes to

[1] The common law of the period.

their land and serfs as an incontestable legal maxim in the face of the whole country. The supreme power, exempt from the sphere of the civil law, interfered, ruling and advising, in all private affairs, and dictated moral duties to parents and children, landowners and servants; they ventured through their all-embracing legislative wisdom to settle every possible lawsuit of the future at the outset.

With this code the old absolutism said its last word: it surrounded its power with fixed barr'ers, raised the commonwealth to a constitutional State; and at the same time it unsuspectingly entered upon the path which must lead to a new juridical union of the German people, in that it destroyed the validity of the Roman law. The mechanical conception of the State of the Frederician period was soon afterwards replaced by a deeply penetrating philosophy, the incomplete jurist training of Carmer and Suarez by the work of historical jurisprudence; but the *Allgemeine Landrecht*[1] nevertheless remained for some decades the firm foundation from which sprang all further reforms of the Prussian State.

The belief in the authority of the law, a preliminary condition of all political freedom, became a living power in the bureaucracy as well as among the people. If the State existed for the general welfare, an irresistible necessity, of which Frederick suspected nothing, led to the desire for the

[1] The common law of the period.

removal of the privileges of the upper classes and the participation of the nation in the government of the State. And sooner or later these conclusions had to be drawn, since already now only the genius and strength of a great man could deal with the difficult problems which this enlarged kingdom presented.

Frederick did not promote the spiritual life of his people to nearly the same extent. We know from Goethe's confessions how fruitfully and in the interests of freedom the heroism of the seven years operated on the German civilization: how in those years of military glory a new import, an increasing sense of vitality, asserted itself in the exhausted literature, how the impoverished language, which had long sought to express mighty sentiments, now at last struggled up out of the insipidity and emptiness and found great words for great emotions: really, the first German comedy, *Minna von Barnhelm*, was created beneath the beating of the drums of the Prussian camp. The Prussian people took a rich share in the wonderful awakening of the spirit, and presented the literary movement with several of its pioneers, from Winckelmann down to Hamann and Herder. And wholly filled with the Prussian spirit was that new maturer form of German Protestantism which at last emerged victoriously out of the philosophical disputes of this "effervescing period" and became a common property of the North-German peoples: the ethics of Kant.

Frederick the Great

The *categorical imperative* of Kant could only be imagined on this ground of Evangelical freedom and faithful self-sacrificing work. Where before rough commands extorted silent submission, now every free judgment was challenged, through the example of the King, who relied fearlessly on the strength of the enquiring mind and gladly confessed: who grumbles the most, goes farthest.

Frederick carried on the old Prussian policy of Christian toleration liberally, and he proclaimed in his code the principle: "The people's conceptions of God and godly things cannot be the subject of a coercive law." Nor did the Free-thinker give up the attempts at union of his ancestors, but strongly maintained that the two Evangelical Churches should not refuse each other the Holy Communion in case of necessity. The supreme ecclesiastical authority of the throne, which he claimed, ensured him against political intrigues on behalf of the clergy, and even allowed him to tolerate in his State the Society of Jesus, suspended by the Pope.

He accorded the Press an almost unlimited freedom, since "newspapers, in order to be interesting, must not be interfered with." He defined all schools as "organizations of the State," and spoke readily and spiritedly of the State's duty to bring up the younger generation to independent thought and a sacrificing love of the Fatherland. He constantly extolled the illustriousness of learning and poetry as the greatest ornament of the kingdom: he showed himself a German and a prince of peace in that he regarded the classics, and not the exact sciences, like the soldier Napoleon, as the spring of all higher education. Nevertheless, the King accomplished very little for the promotion of national education directly.

The scarcity of money, the lack of competent board-school teachers, and the unceasing struggles now with foreign enemies, now with the economic question at home, rendered the carrying out of his plans more difficult; and in the end the dry utilitarianism of the father always broke out again in the son. This economical Prince would provide means for anything rather than for the purposes of instruction.

When the Germans in the Empire sneered that this Prussia had starved itself into greatness, they thought chiefly of the Prussian teachers and scholars. Only what was absolutely necessary was done for the national schools; the repeatedly enjoined discipline of compulsory general attendance at school remained a dead letter for wide stretches of the country. None of the Prussian Universities attained the fame of the new *Georgia Augusta*.[1] Only towards the end of the Frederician period, when Zedlitz, the friend of Kant, took over the direction of the educational organizations, did a somewhat freer impulse enter into the public instruction. At that time the worthy Abbot Felbiger reformed the Catholic national

[1] The University at Göttingen, named after its founder.

schools, and found enthusiastic supporters in the Empire, so that in the end Catholic Germany participated in the greatest blessing of the Reformation.

It seemed an easy thing to gather in Berlin a brilliant circle of the best intellects of Germany for pregnant activity. Every young genius in the Empire angled for the eye of the national hero. Even Winckelmann, who had once fled from the country in hot hatred, now experienced with what strong bands this State fettered the hearts of its sons. "For the first time," he wrote, "the voice of the Fatherland makes itself heard within me, which was unknown to me before." He burned with an eager desire to show the Aristotle of military art that a born subject could achieve something worthy, and negotiated for years for an appointment in Berlin.

But in Frederick's French academy there was no place for German thinkers. The Medicean days, which one had once awaited from the inspired Prince of the Rheinsberger Parnassus, only came for the foreign intellects at the table of Sans Souci; the pupil of French culture would not and could not understand the young unruly life which stirred in the depths of his own people. While the Berliner company intoxicated themselves to overrefinement with the idea of the new literature, and jeering scepticism and refined epicureanism were almost crowding out the old strict moral simplicity, the Prussian administration maintained their one-sided utilitarian bias which only troubled itself about everyday matters. That intolerably stiff, home-baked, prosaic spirit which was instilled into the State of the old Soldier-King was somewhat humanized by Frederick but not broken; only the baroque glory of the New Palace and the mighty cupolas of the *Gensdarmenkirche*[1] made it possible to recognize that at least the barbaric culture-hatred of the thirties had begun gradually to give way.

But still the Prussian State represented only the one half of our national life; the delicacy and the yearning, the profoundness and the enthusiasm of the German character, could not obtain just recognition in this prosaic world. The centre-point of the German policy was not the home of the intellectual work of the nation; the classical period of our poetry found its scene of action in the minor States.

In this momentous fact lies the key to many puzzles of modern German history. To the coolly averted attitude of King Frederick our Literature owes the most precious thing it possesses—its unequalled freedom; but this indifference of the

[1] I cannot find out about this anywhere, but there is the Gensdarmenmarkt, with the French Church and the New Church, because Frederick was fond of French things. But in Baedeker, it does not say anything about the change of name, though it does say that the two churches with the theatre form the finest group of buildings in Berlin. In an 1893 Baedeker, it says that they are of the last century, which would make it about the time.—L. S.

Crown of Prussia during the days which decided the character of modern German culture was to blame for the fact that it was for a long time difficult for the heroes of German thought to understand the one vital State in Germany. After Frederick's death two full decades elapsed before Prussia gave hospitable reception to the intellectual powers of the new Germany; and then more long decades passed before German learning recognized that it was of one blood with the Prussian State, that the State-organizing power of our people had its root in the same strong idealism which inspired the German intellectual curiosity and artistic industry to bold daring.

Frederick's coldness towards German culture is perhaps the saddest, the most unnatural phenomenon in the long history of the suffering of modern Germany. The first man of the nation, who awakened again in the Germans the courage to believe in themselves, was quite a stranger to the noblest and most characteristic works of his people; it cannot be expressed too clearly and strongly, how slowly and with what difficulty this people threw off the hard inheritance of the thirty years, the spiritual supremacy of the foreigner.

Frederick was not, like Henry IV of France, a faithful representative of the national vices and virtues, intelligible to the national disposition in every undulation of his mood. Two natures struggled within him: the philosophical scholar, who revelled in the sound of music, in the melody of French verse, who considered poetical fame the greatest happiness on earth, who cried to his Voltaire in honest admiration: "Destiny bestowed on me the empty show of rank, on you every talent; the better portion is yours"—and the robust North-German man, who stormed at his Brandenburgers with rough Brandenburg *Jod*,[1] a model of martial courage, restless energy, and iron severity, for the stern, austere people.

The French enlightenment of the eighteenth century was tainted with a deep insincerity: it had neither the will nor the strength to make the life agree with the idea: people raved of the holy simplicity of Nature, and were unutterably pleased with the most unnatural customs and costumes which ever governed the European world; people jeered at the absurd chance of birth, dreamed of the original freedom and equality, and yet lived gaily on in an insolent contempt of humanity, and all the sweet sins of the old fawning society, borne up with the hope that sometime in a distant future Reason would set up her throne on the fragments of all existing things.

At the Prussian Court, witty, malicious Prince Henry was a faithful representative of this new culture; theoretically a disdainer of that empty smoke, which is called fame and power by the mob, practically a man of hard and fast conception of political rulership, unscrupulous, versed

[1] Idiom.

in all tricks and intrigues. And Frederick, too, in his way, led this double life of the men of the French enlightenment.[1] His was that tragic fate to think and to speak in two languages, neither of which did he absolutely master. The crude gibberish which was shouted at the *Tabakskollegium* (smoking club, or the Tobacco Parliament of Frederick William I of Prussia) of his father seemed to the beauty-intoxicated youth just as offensive as the ponderous literary German of the learned pedantism which he came to know from the works of orthodox theologians; good or evil, he contented himself with this clumsy language, discharged passing business now in rough dialect, now in stiff pulpit-style.

For the world of ideas, with which his head bubbled over, he found worthy expression only in the language of cosmopolitan culture. He knew well that his bizarre and Teutonic[2] Muse spoke a barbaric French, and in the consciousness of this weakness estimated the art-worth of his verses at a lower value than they deserved. The one thing, at least, which makes the poet, the protean gift, was in no way denied him. His Muse commanded the whole scale of emotions; she now expressed with lofty earnestness the great and noble, now, in a satirical mood, with the mischievousness of an elf—or, to tell the truth, with the

---

[1] The period of Voltaire, the period preceding the Revolution, humanistic in character.
[2] In the original "tudesque."

mischievousness of a Berlin street-arab—teased and tormented her victim. And yet instinct tells him that the richness of his mind does not flow so full and clear in his verses as in the notes of his flute; the fullest melody, the deepest feeling were unattainable to the German in the foreign language.

The philosopher of Sans Souci never became quite at home in the foreign culture which he so earnestly admired. Above all, the strictness of his moral conception of the world divided him from his French companions. It is the greatness of Protestantism, that it imperiously commands or requires the unity of thought and will, the unity of the religious and moral life.

Frederick's moral training was too deeply rooted in the German Protestant life not to perceive the secret weakness of the French philosophy. He viewed the Church with a more liberal mind than the Catholic Voltaire, who, in his *Henriade*, the gospel of the new toleration, in the end arrived at the conclusion that all respectable people should belong to the Roman Church; he had never, as Voltaire, bowed his neck to religious forms which his conscience condemned, and could endure with the calm serenity of the born heretic the fact that the Roman Curia placed his works on the Index of forbidden books. Although he from time to time condescendingly defined philosophy as his hobby, yet the reflection on the great problems of existence was far more to him than an ingenious pastime; in the fashion of the ancients, he sought and found in intellectual work the rest of the mind at peace with itself, that lofty superiority of the soul to all vicissitudes of fortune.

After the errors of his passionate youth, he soon learned to subdue that impulse of artistic tenderness and sensuality, which threatened to drive him to epicurean pleasures. Boldly as scorn and scepticism stirred in his head, the moral order of the Universe, the idea of duty, remained inviolable to him. The terrible earnestness of his life, wholly dedicated to duty, was divided as by all the breadth of heaven from the effeminate and loose morals of the Parisian enlightenment. As his writings —in that clear and sharp style, which at times becomes trivial, but never vague—always irresistibly aimed at a certain decided and palpable conclusion, so he wished to fashion his life according to what he recognized as truth; as far as the opposition of a barbaric world allowed, he sought to ensure in State and Society a humane conception of things, which he called the cardinal virtue of every thinking being, and went to meet death with the calm consciousness "of leaving the world loaded with my good deeds."

For all that, he never succeeded in wholly overcoming the duality of his mind. The struggle within betrays itself in Frederick's biting wit, which came out so harshly because the hero in his arrogant directness never thought of hiding it. The life of genius is always mysterious, but seldom does it appear so difficult to understand as in the richness of this dual mind. The King looks down with superior irony on the coarse ignorance of his Brandenburg nobility; he breathes freely when he can refresh himself from the boredom of this unintellectual company with the one man to whom he looks up admiringly, the Master of the French poetry; at the same time he recognized what he owed to the sword of that rude race, he could not find sufficient words to praise the courage, the fidelity, the honourableness of his nobility; he curbs his jeering before the stern Biblical faith of old Zieten. The French are welcome guests for the cheerful after-dinner hours; his respect belongs to the Germans.

No one of the foreign companions got so near to the heart of Frederick as that "Seelenmensch"[1] Winterfeldt, who courageously maintained his German nature even against his royal friend. In his letters Frederick often yearned for the new Athens away on the Seine, and bewailed the envy of jealous gods, who had condemned the son of the Muse to rule over slaves in the Cimmerian land of the North. And yet he shared as patiently as his father the troubles and cares of this wretched people, glad from the bottom of his heart of the new life which was springing up under the rough fists of his peasants, and cried proudly: "I prefer our simplicity, even our poverty, to those damned riches which corrupt the dignity of our race."

[1] A man of great feeling and tactful understanding.

Woe to the foreign poets if they presumed to give the King political advice; hard and scornful he waved them back to the limits of their art.

Vigorously as he was occupied with the ideas of the modern France, he was only a great author when he was expressing German thoughts in French words, when he spoke as a German Prince and General in his political, military, and historical works. Not in the foreign school, but through his own strength and an unrivalled experience, Frederick became the first publicist of our eighteenth century, the only German who approached the State with creative criticism, and spoke of the duties of the citizen in lofty style: no one before of that people without a country had known how to speak so warmly and deeply as the author of the *Letters of Philopatros* about the love of the Fatherland.

The old King no longer considered it worth the trouble to climb down from the height of his French Parnassus into the lowlands of the German Muse, and judge with his own eyes whether the poetical art of his people was not awakened at last. In his essays on German Literature, six years before his death, he repeated the old impeachment of the fastidious Parisian critic against the undisciplined wildness of the German language, and dismissed the horrible platitudes of *Götz von Berlichingen*, which he had hardly read, with words of contempt. And yet this infamous discussion itself gives an eloquent proof of the passionate national pride of the hero. He prophesied for the future of Germany a period of intellectual fame, which already irradiated the unsuspecting nation with its dawning glory. As Moses he sees the Promised Land lying in the distance, and concludes hopefully: "Perhaps the late-comers will surpass all their predecessors." So close and so distant, so foreign and so familiar, was the relationship of Germany's greatest King to his people.

The great period of the old monarchy was setting. Round the King it became more and more silent; the heroes who had fought his battles, the friends who had laughed and revelled with him, sank one after the other into the grave; loneliness, the curse of the great, came over him. He was never accustomed to spare with his irony any single human emotion; for all the rapturous dreams of his own youth had been trampled underfoot by his pitiless father. In old age inconsiderate austerity became inexorable harshness. The stern old man, who in his rare leisure hours paced along the picture-gallery at Sans Souci with his greyhounds, or in the round temple of the Park dwelt dejectedly on his dead sister, saw far beneath his feet a new generation of tiny human beings growing up around him: they must fear him and obey him; he was indifferent to their love. The preponderance of one man weighed oppressively on the people. On the rare occasions when he went to the Opera House, opera and the singers seemed to the audience to be swallowed up; everyone gazed towards that place in the *parterre* where sat the failing old man, with the large, hard eyes. When the news of his death came, a Swabian peasant, from the hearts of countless Germans, cried: "Who will rule the world now?"

To his last breath all the will-power of the Prussian Monarchy emanated from this one man; the day of his death was the first day of rest of his life. His will told the nation once more how differently from the domestic politics of the minor courts was the Hohenzollerns' idea of kingship: "My last wishes at the moment of my death will concern the happiness of this State; may it be the happiest of States through the mildness of its laws, the most justly administered in its internal affairs, the most valiantly defended by an army which breathes only honour and noble fame, and may it last and flourish until the end of time."

A century and a half had elapsed since a Frederick William sought among the fragments of the old Empire the first materials for the building of the modern Great Power. Hundreds of thousands of Prussians had found a hero's death, colossal labour had been expended on the establishment of the new German kingdom, and at least one rich blessing of these terrible struggles was felt forcibly in the Empire: the nation felt at home again, mistress on her own soil. A long-missed feeling of safety beautified life for the Germans in the Empire; it seemed to them as if this Prussia was destined by Nature to protect the peaceful industries of the nation with its shield against all foreign disturbers. Without this strong feeling of national ease our German poetry would never have found the joyous courage to achieve great things.

Public opinion began gradually to be reconciled to the State which had grown up against their will; one took it up as a necessity of German life, without troubling much about its future. The difficult question: how such a bold conception of the State could be maintained without the invigorating strength of genius?—was only seriously raised by one contemporary, by Mirabeau. The old and new epochs gave each other a friendly greeting once more, when the tribune of the approaching revolution stayed at Sans Souci, shortly before the death of the King. With the glowing colour-splendour of his rhetoric, Mirabeau portrayed the greatest man he had ever beheld; he called Frederick's State a truly noble work of art, the one State of the present which could seriously occupy a brilliant mind; but it did not escape him that this daring building unfortunately rested on much too weak a foundation. The Prussians of those days could not understand such uncertainty; the glory of the Frederician epoch seemed so wonderful that even this most fault-finding of all European peoples was blinded by it.

For the next generation the fame of Frederick proved fatal; men lived in delusive security, and forgot that only renewed hard labour could uphold the work of unutterable toil. But when the days of shame and trial came, the Prussian again experienced the surviving efficacy of Genius; the memory of Rossbach and Leuthen was the last moral force which kept the leaking ship of the German Monarchy above water; and when the State once more took up arms for the struggle of despair, a South-German poet saw the figure of the great King descend from the clouds, and call to the people: "Up, my Prussians! Under my flag! and you shall be greater than your ancestors!"

TREITSCHKE AS A HISTORIAN

LORD ACTON says of Treitschke:
"He is the one writer of history who is more brilliant and more powerful than Droysen: he writes with the force and incisiveness of Mommsen."

HEINRICH VON TREITSCHKE (1834–1896) was a Saxon who in 1863 became Professor at Freiburg, in Baden, and in 1866 became a Prussian subject and editor of the *Preussische Jahrbücher*. After being a Professor at Kiel and Heidelberg, in 1874 he became Professor at Berlin. From 1871 he was a Member of the Reichstag. At first a Liberal, he became the chief panegyrist of the House of Hohenzollern. According to the *Encyclopædia Britannica:* "He did more than anyone to mould the minds of the rising generation, and he carried them with him even in his violent attacks on all opinions and all parties which appeared in any way to be injurious to the rising power of Germany. He supported the Government in its attempts to subdue by legislation the Socialists, Poles, and Catholics; and he was one of the few men of eminence who gave the sanction of his name to the attacks on the Jews which began in 1878. As a strong advocate of colonial expansion he was also a bitter enemy of Great Britain, and he was to a large extent responsible for the anti-British feeling into which so much of German Chauvinism was directed during the last years of the nineteenth century."

"As a historian," says the *E. B.*, "Treitschke holds a very high place. His work, indeed, lies entirely in the history of the last two centuries. He approached history as a politician; he had none of the passion for research for its own sake, and confined himself to those periods and characters in which great political problems were being worked out; above all, he was a patriotic historian, and he never wandered far from Prussia. His great achievement was the *History of Germany in the Nineteenth Century.* The first volume was published in 1879, and during the next sixteen years four more volumes appeared, but at his death he had only advanced to the year 1847. It will remain a fragment, and it is much to be regretted that he did not live to complete the account of the Revolution, in which he would have had a subject worthy of his peculiar powers. The work shows extreme diligence, scrupulous care in the use of authorities, and in the years he covered he has left little for future historians to discover. It is too discursive and is badly arranged, but it is marked by a power of style, a vigour of narrative, and a skill in delineation of character which give life to the most unattractive period of German history; notwithstanding the extreme spirit of partisanship and some faults of taste, it will remain a remarkable monument of literary ability. Besides this he wrote a number of biographical and historical essays, as well as numerous articles and papers on questions rising out of contemporary politics, of which some are valuable contributions to political thought, while others are political controversy not always of the best kind."

www.ingramcontent.com/pod-product-compliance
Lightning Source LLC
Chambersburg PA
CBHW032108090426
42743CB00007B/275